► Family Language Policy

DOI: 10.1057/9781137521811.0001

Other Palgrave Pivot titles

palgrave▸pivot

Family Language Policy: Maintaining an Endangered Language in the Home

Cassie Smith-Christmas

University of the Highlands and Islands/University of Edinburgh, UK

DOI: 10.1057/9781137521811.0001

First published 2016 by
PALGRAVE MACMILLAN

Palgrave Macmillan in the UK is an imprint of Macmillan Publishers Limited, registered in England, company number 785998, of Houndmills, Basingstoke, Hampshire RG21 6XS.

Palgrave Macmillan in the US is a division of St Martin's Press LLC, 175 Fifth Avenue, New York, NY 10010.

Palgrave Macmillan is the global academic imprint of the above companies and has companies and representatives throughout the world.

Palgrave® and Macmillan® are registered trademarks in the United States, the United Kingdom, Europe and other countries.

ISBN: 978–1–137–52182–8   EPUB
ISBN: 978–1–137–52181–1   PDF
ISBN: 978–1–137–52180–4   Hardback

A catalogue record for this book is available from the British Library.

A catalog record for this book is available from the Library of Congress.

www.palgrave.com/pivot

DOI: 10.1057/9781137521811

► *For Nana and her family*

DOI: 10.1057/9781137521811.0001

Contents

DOI: 10.1057/9781137521811.0001

DOI: 10.1057/9781137521811.0001

List of Conversation Examples

DOI: 10.1057/9781137521811.0002

Preface

The moment the bus turned the corner on its final leg of the long journey from Glasgow to Skye, I began to wave at a woman on a bench near the bus stop. It felt like such a natural reaction on seeing her, but I don't know why – I had never seen her in my life and there were a few other women that matched the age of the woman I was coming to meet – but I just waved anyway, and the woman started waving back. I was wearing my red jacket, as I said I would in my e-mail, so she must have known it was me, and when I stepped off the bus, she wrapped me in her arms and said, 'Welcome Cassie.' And thus began my friendship with the Campbell family. Little did Nana – the woman waiting for me at the bus stop – know that by answering my letter to the editor in the *West Highland Free Press* looking for three generations of a Gaelic-speaking family that she would be landed with a linguist indefinitely (as my original plan was to stay ten days!). And neither could I have known how much my own life was about to change by meeting Nana and her family. But I think at that moment I did have a glimpse of how lucky I was to find Nana and that feeling of luck and gratitude has continued. As these pages will show, Nana and her family have shown me the upmost generosity in letting me into their home to, as they sometimes joke, 'spy' on their language practices. I am so very grateful to them and am honoured to tell their story, of how they are trying to keep their endangered language alive, and how sadly, despite their best efforts, it remains an uphill struggle.

DOI: 10.1057/9781137521811.0003

Personal Acknowledgements

First of all, thank you to Nana and her family, without whom this book would not be possible. Thank you to Dick Smakman for encouraging me to embark on the study that led me to the Campbell family in the first place and to Nancy Dorian for sending me her 1974 and 1976 test sentences, without which this study would not have been possible. Thank you to Roibeard Ó Maolalaigh and Jane Stuart-Smith for supervising my PhD thesis on language practices in the Campbell family and thank you as well to my friends and colleagues at the University of Glasgow for their support over the years. I would also like to acknowledge the financial support given by St Andrew's Society and the CGA for my PhD research and also to Soillse for financial support for recording and transcribing the 2014 corpus. Thank you as well to Soillse and the University of the Highlands and Islands for supporting my research fellowship and to my friends and colleagues in Soillse, especially to Timothy Currie Armstrong, Stuart Dunmore, who transcribed a large part of the 2014 corpus, and Wilson McLeod, who kindly read a draft of this book. I am also indebted to the Institute of the Advanced Studies in the Humanities (IASH) at the University of Edinburgh for providing such a stimulating environment in which to write this book and thanks to my friends and colleagues at IASH for making this such a fruitful fellowship. Thank you as well to the many friends and colleagues who have commented on my work over the years at various events. Thanks also to Åsa Palviainen and the other organisers and participants of the family

DOI: 10.1057/9781137521811.0004

language policy workshop in Jyväskylä and especially to Alison Crump and Josep Cru for feedback on various stages of this manuscript. Any mistakes are of course my own.

Finally, thank you to my parents and also to my brother, who passed away in 2010, but who nonetheless is part of all I do, now and forever.

DOI: 10.1057/9781137521811.0004

Key to Transcript Conventions Used

:	elongated sound
-	cut-off
<u>word</u>	emphasis
WORD	increased amplitude
°	decreased amplitude
HI<	higher pitch
WH<	whispered
CR<	creaky voice
BR<	breathy voice
> <	accelerated speech
=	latching speech
[[ ]	overlapping speech
(.5)	pause (seconds)
(.)	micropause (less than two-tenths of a second)
@	laughter (pulse)
(( ))	non-verbal action
{ }	word/sound said ingressively
/	rising pitch
\	falling pitch
/\	rise/fall pitch
.hh	egressive sound
(?)	uncertainty in transcript
•	turns omitted

DOI: 10.1057/9781137521811.0005

1
What Is Family Language Policy?

Abstract: *This chapter traces Family Language Policy (FLP) research from its origins in sociolinguistic approaches to child bilingualism and details how examining language input both in terms of* quantity *and* quality *has been central to elucidating the fundamental question of why some children attain greater competency in their minority language than others. It also highlights the importance of discussing this question in relation to different contexts, such as language shift situations either involving an immigrant or autochthonous minority language community. The chapter concludes by briefly introducing the 'Campbell family,' who are the locus of this particular FLP study and gives a brief background to their minority language (Scottish Gaelic) as well as the area in which they live (Isle of Skye).*

Keywords: child bilingualism; Family Language Policy; language shift; Scottish Gaelic

Smith-Christmas, Cassie. *Family Language Policy: Maintaining an Endangered Language in the Home.* Basingstoke: Palgrave Macmillan, 2016. DOI: 10.1057/9781137521811.0006.

OPOL origins and the importance of input

Within the last decade, the term 'Family Language Policy' ('FLP') has gained increasing currency within sociolinguistic literature, largely due to the efforts of Kendall King and Lyn Fogle in delimiting FLP as a field in its own right (King and Fogle, 2006; King, Fogle, and Logan-Terry, 2008; Fogle and King, 2013; King and Fogle, 2013). Underlying the development of this field is the fundamental question of why some children being raised in bi/multilingual environments achieve relatively equal competence in their minority language (the lesser-used language in the child's sociocultural environment) as they do in their dominant language (the majority language of a particular area, which often equates to a national and/or official language). Early academic interest in this question can be traced back to the 1902 publication of Maurice Grammont's *Observations sur le langage des enfants* (*Observations on Children's Language*), which is credited with introducing the concept of *une personne une langue* (one-person one-language), which in current FLP research has come to mean the 'one-*parent* one-language' strategy (abbreviated OPOL). A few years later, Grammont's friend Ronjat, a French linguist living in Paris whose wife was German, used this method in raising his son. In 1913 Ronjat published an account of the child's French-German development from birth to age 4;10 (four years and ten months). Ronjat and his wife each used only their native language when addressing their son and Ronjat reported that his son attained proficiency similar to that of a native monolingual in both languages. The OPOL method was then later documented in Leopold's (1939–1949) longitudinal study of his daughter Hildegard, who was growing up with a German-speaking father (the author of the study) and an English-speaking mother in the United States. Like Ronjat, Leopold also reported success in using the OPOL strategy. However, when Hildegard progressed to adolescence, she became reluctant to use German in her American-dominated life; further, Hildegard's younger sister did not attain the same German fluency that Hildegard had achieved in her early years (see Barron-Hauwaert [2004] for a more thorough overview on OPOL studies).

Following these two landmark studies, there was a nearly 30 year hiatus in studies which take a sociolinguistic approach to child bilingualism. However, the 1980s saw the beginning of renewed interest in this vein of inquiry; monographs such as Fantini (1985), Döpke (1992), de Houwer (1990) and Lanza (1997) were instrumental in forging the path

DOI: 10.1057/9781137521811.0006

to a renewed interest in child bilingualism, a path which has continued to expand in the last three decades. This continuing research into child bilingualism has not only been instrumental in expanding knowledge about child language development in general, but has also been important in debunking popular myths about bilingualism, such as, for example, the misconception that bilingualism impedes the child's intellectual development (for example, Anastasi and Cordova, 1953). Further, as Grosjean (1992) points out, bilingualism research has often been constrained within a monolingual framework – for example, by focusing on bilinguals solely in terms of their monolingual competencies – and research into child bilingualism has widened this monolingual-centred perspective.

In terms of the central question of why some children attain higher levels of fluency in the minority language than others, several key factors have been identified. One factor is the overall amount of minority language input the child receives. Perhaps not surprisingly, children who receive more minority language input tend to be more productive bilinguals than children who receive less minority language input (Döpke, 1988; de Houwer, 2007; Quiroz, Snow, and Zhao, 2010). The amount of input may vary for a number of reasons; for example, the amount of time the child spends with the minority language-speaking caregiver might be a significant factor. Lyon (1996) and Varro (1998) for instance conclude that having a mother who speaks the minority language may be a predictor of minority language maintenance, as typically mothers tend to be children's primary caregivers. The total quantity of input may also be affected by exposure to other minority language-speaking caregivers such as grandparents, aunts and uncles, as well as child minders (Bayley, Schecter, and Torres-Ayala, 1996; Kenner, Ruby, Jessel, Gregory, and Arju, 2007; Ruby, 2012; Kopeliovich, 2013; Melo-Pfeifer, 2014; Pillai, Soh, and Kajita, 2014). Typically, as noted in Leopold's study and discussed more recently in Döpke (1992) and Dumanig, David, and Shanmuganathan (2013), older children tend to receive more overall minority language input than their younger siblings and therefore achieve higher levels of competency in the minority language. However, as Schwartz (2010, p. 173) points out, this is not necessarily a reality in all multilingual families. In Yates and Terraschke's (2013) study of immigrant families in Australia, for example, older siblings born in the home country had a positive impact on their younger siblings' minority language input. The contextual nature of the relationship between input and older siblings is also clearly illustrated

DOI: 10.1057/9781137521811.0006

in Kopeliovich's (2013) longitudinal study of her own four children's Russian-Hebrew development. Kopeliovich's eldest child's early years were largely experienced as monolingual Russian, as both Kopeliovich and her husband spoke exclusively Russian in their home in Israel and the child's Russian-speaking grandparents also frequently looked after him. However, the next two children's experiences were different, as by then the eldest child began using Hebrew in the home. Subsequently, the second child then began to use Hebrew with the third child. This situation reversed, however, at the birth of the fourth child, as all the older children spoke Russian to the fourth child, thus significantly increasing the minority language input the fourth child received.

The different outcomes in terms of older siblings' impact on younger siblings' language use demonstrates the highly dynamic and contextual nature of different factors in terms of overall language input. However, as Mishina-Mori (2011) points out, high levels of home input do not necessarily result in minority language maintenance and the question of the *quality* of the input (usually in conjunction with examinations of overall *quantity* of input) has become equally important in exploring why some children attain higher fluency in the minority language than others. The question of quality has centred mainly on the more socio-linguistic and especially interactional aspects of input, not necessarily the linguistic aspects (though see Evans, 1987). On a very general level and also related to the premise that greater input equals higher competence, Kasuya (1998) finds that parental input consistency – for example, refraining from code-switching – is an important factor in the children's use of the minority language (though see Patterson's [1999] questioning of this general premise). Equally, input quality in terms of different registers may also be an integral factor, as Stavans (2012) shows with the importance of narratives in the successful FLPs of Ethiopians in Israel. Related to register is also the matter of style; Takeuchi's (2006) study of Japanese mothers in Australia for example finds that use of a style which encourages the child's active participation in the conversation is integral to language maintenance. Similarly, Döpke (1992) finds that language maintenance may hinge on the degree to which a particular interaction is 'child-centred,' in other words, interactions which engage the child in activities such as play and storytime. In Döpke's landmark study of OPOL German-English families in Australia, the children with German-speaking fathers evidence more productive use of German than children with German-speaking mothers. Döpke attributes this finding

DOI: 10.1057/9781137521811.0006

to the impact of gender roles on interaction type and consequently the child's experience of the minority language; in general, the families followed traditional parental roles – in other words, the mother stayed home with children – and therefore the children with German-speaking mothers' exposure to the minority language covered a broad range of mundane household activities, including disciplining, while the children with German-speaking fathers' experience of the minority language was more explicitly child-centred.

Lanza's (1997) work on two OPOL English-Norwegian families is another landmark study in terms of elucidating the important relationship between the qualitative components of input and the child's success in the minority language. Lanza's analysis takes a child language socialisation perspective, which views the acquisition of language as a process embedded in, not separate from, the child's developing understanding of culturally appropriate norms (see Schiefflin and Ochs, 1984, 1986; Ochs, 1993; Duranti, Ochs, and Schiefflin, 2011). In terms of a child being raised in a bilingual and/or multilingual environment, this understanding is comprised of an understanding of *who* uses a particular language, *to whom* it should be used, *where* it should be used, and also whether or not it is appropriate to *mix* the two languages. Lanza surmises that parents who enforce strict boundaries in terms of each language's appropriateness at a given time negotiate more monolingual-centred contexts for interaction and in doing so, more adequately ensure the child's development in the minority language. Lanza (p. 262) identifies five main ways a caregiver can respond to the child's inappropriate code use and lists them on a continuum from negotiating a monolingual context to negotiating a bilingual context. In using the first (and most monolingual) strategy, *Request for Clarification: Minimal Grasp Strategy*, the parent explicitly asks the child to repeat the utterance, implying that the utterance is in some way 'faultable' (*cf.* Goffman, 1981) and therefore requires what in Conversational Analytic (CA) terms is referred to as a 'repair.' This strategy allows the parent to feign monolingualism in one language, a tactic which Lanza notes has been found to be successful in other studies (for example, Taeschner, 1983). The second-most monolingually oriented strategy is the *Request for Clarification: Expressed Guess Strategy*, in which the parent poses a question in Language A to reformulate what the child has said in Language B. This strategy does not allow the parent to feign monolingualism, as it is clear that the parent at least has passive knowledge of Language B, but using a question allows for the child's utterance

DOI: 10.1057/9781137521811.0006

to be marked as faultable and also allows for the child to repair his or her utterance using the appropriate code. The third strategy is *Repetition*, in which the parent repeats in Language A what the child says in Language B. This is less overt in marking the child's utterance as faultable, as it does not implicitly request a response from the child in Language A. In the fourth strategy, the *Move on Strategy*, the child's use of Language B is simply glossed over and the parent continues in Language A with no implicit requests that the child use Language A (*cf.* Saville-Troike's [1987] 'dual-lingual' paradigm; also Gafaranga's [2010] concept of 'parallel mode'). Finally, the last strategy is *Code-Switching*, where the caregiver either uses intrasentential code-switching by incorporating the child's utterance in Language B into the parent's use of Language A, or by using intersentential code-switching and switching to Language B in his or her next utterance.

FLP from a language shift perspective

The sub-strategy (intersentential code-switching) in Lanza's (1997) paradigm is analogous to what Gafaranga (2010, 2011) refers to as 'talking language shift into being' in discussing the language practices of the Rwandan community in Belgium. 'Talking language shift into being' occurs when the adult's first pair-part (in other words, the initial statement or question that requires a response; *cf.* Sacks, Schegloff, and Jefferson, 1974) in the minority code is met with the child's second pair-part in the majority code and the adult then switches to the majority code for his or her subsequent conversational turn. Gafaranga argues that the accumulation of this practice at the micro-level can result in a shift to the majority language over time. Gafaranga's articles are emblematic of the fact that studies of child language use and development in an immigrant community are often also by nature studies of *language shift*, the process by which a group of speakers cease speaking their own language in favour of the majority language. As renowned pioneer in the field Joshua Fishman (1991) emphasises, the successful maintenance of a community's language hinges on the successful transmission of the language in the home, which is Stage 6 in his well-known Graded Intergenerational Disruption Scale (GIDS) and which he also refers to the 'fulcrum' (2001, p. 467) in terms of Reversing Language Shift (RLS). In earlier work, Fishman (1971) postulates that within no more than three

DOI: 10.1057/9781137521811.0006

generations of leaving their home country, immigrants to the United States will have undergone language shift and will only speak the majority language. This three-generational paradigm has been instrumental in other studies examining language shift and the family, highlighted for example by Li Wei's (1994) well-known monograph on Chinese-speaking families in Tyneside, England, titled *Three Generations, Two Languages, One Family*. This and earlier work (Li Wei, Milroy, and Pong Sin Ching 1992) highlights how language shift in the family and within the wider community is a reflexive process; that is, shift in one domain exacerbates shift in the other domain. In his study of language use among families in the Tamil diaspora, Canagarajah (2008, p. 173) also emphasises the reflexive nature of community and family, writing:

> We find that the family is not self-contained, closed off to other social institutions and economic conditions. Furthermore, the family is shaped by history and power, at times reproducing ideological values and power inequalities established from colonial times. Such a broadened perspective is critical to theorizing the prospects of the family in maintaining a marginalized language.

Canagarajah's point highlights one of the key differences between studies of language use in the family from an OPOL perspective and studies of language use in the family from the perspective of an immigrant community undergoing shift. Fundamentally, both these types of studies are asking the same question – why do some children acquire the minority language while others fail to do so – but the contexts are very different. As Kirsch (2012) points out, OPOL studies tend to centre on contexts where the 'minority' language is actually a majority (and prestigious) language in its own right – for example, English in Norway. Although of course in OPOL studies usually at least one of the parents is an immigrant, the distinction is drawn here between prototypical OPOL studies, which, as Döpke (1998, p. 3) emphasises, tend to focus on middle-class parents, and studies in which there is a community of immigrants (Rwandans in Belgium; Chinese in England) who are a collective minority vis-à-vis the dominant culture and who normally have less social capital than members of the dominant culture. Thus although certainly the languages of immigrant community studies may also be majority languages in their own right – for example, Mandarin in Li Wei's study – the context of belonging to an immigrant group means that the speakers and therefore their language most likely does not afford the same prestige as do the

DOI: 10.1057/9781137521811.0006

'minority' languages in OPOL studies. Further, because of this asymmetrical social status of the immigrant group, immigrant parents are more likely to be told by members of the majority language society, such as teachers and school officials, not to speak their own language to their children because it will impede the child's integration and/or academic development. In OPOL studies, the child's lack of minority use is usually not attributed to the stigmatisation of their language and culture, but is normally put down to factors *within* the family, such as the contexts in which the child interacts with the minority language-speaking parents, or the overall amount of input in the home. In studies of immigrant communities, however, wider societal factors external to the family, such as the pressure to integrate or the stigmatisation of the minority culture, may be important factors in explaining why the child evidences low use of the minority language.

Like immigrant community studies of language use in the family, studies of autochthonous minority language communities – that is communities whose minority language owes its status to the encroachment of another community upon the minority community, often in the form of colonisation – also focus on the reflexive relationship between family and a wider sociocultural and historical context. Just as external pressures from the dominant culture may force the minority immigrant culture to abandon its language in order to integrate or alleviate stigmatisation, so too may autochthonous minority communities abandon their language for similar reasons (for example, see Dorian, 1981; Hill, 1983; Schmidt, 1985; Dauenhauer and Dauenhauer, 1998; McCarty, Romero-Little, and Zepeda, 2008; see also Fishman, 1991). In autochthonous communities, however, the factors underlying the overall shift to the majority language may have been in place for centuries rather than generations; in turn, studies that examine the intersection of language shift and FLP often show how normalisation of language shift at the community level translates into practices that further perpetuate this shift at the micro-level of family interactions. For example, in his well-known ethnography of the remote village of Gapun, Papua New Guinea, and Kulick (1992, p. 215) postulates that one of the many factors contributing to the rapid language shift from the local Taiap to the dominant Tok Pisin is that 'the association between children and Tok Pisin is, in fact, so strong that adults will address children in that language even if a child should actually happen to answer in Taiap.' The reality of shift and its role in reflexively perpetuating further shift is also discussed in Meek's (2007)

DOI: 10.1057/9781137521811.0006

study of the Kaska community in the Yukon Territory, Canada, which shows how the association of Kaska with elders and those in authority is a significant contributing factor to the children's reluctance to use the minority language. Makihara (2005) however demonstrates that the realities of language shift may not necessarily reflexively work to perpetuate further shift. In her study of family language practices on Easter Island, she shows how children's insertion of Rapa Nui into Spanish as a way to mark cultural identity means that although the children are still dominant in Spanish, on some level they maintain their minority language Rapa Nui. Although Makihara concedes that proponents of language maintenance may in fact see this as furthering the language's decline (particularly those who subscribe to more purist language ideologies), she argues that this 'ideology of inclusiveness' (p. 754) may be a contributing factor in slowing the language's decline; by using what Rapa Nui they *do* speak, the children may be more apt to continue its use or build on their existing competence. She concludes the article by discussing the potential role that Rapa Nui immersion education programmes may play in this process.

The role of *language policy* in an evolving paradigm

This intersection of the community and family through autochthonous minority language education is discussed in detail in Luykx's (2003) study of Aymara households in Bolivia, which to the best of my knowledge, is the first articulation of the term 'Family Language Policy' as such (p. 39):

> While these efforts [minority language schools] are laudable ... , it is the gradual displacement of Aymara by Spanish in functions that have traditionally been the former's stronghold (i.e. the domestic ones) that may prove definitive for the future survival of the language. For this reason, it is necessary to expand our current conception of 'language policy' to include not only the sphere or official state actions, but also decisions made at the community and family level. Such decisions are often implicit and unconscious, but they are no less crucial to determining the speed and direction of language shift. In this regard we may refer to *family language policy* as an important area for both research and activism.

Luykx's framing of the field 'Family Language Policy' in terms of official language policy at the state level, as well as its relationship to education,

DOI: 10.1057/9781137521811.0006

are important aspects in tracing the development of the FLP field as a whole. Recently, FLP research has turned its attention to the critical role that the school may play in the child's minority language development. This is particularly evident in the most recent collected volume devoted to FLP research, titled *Family Language Policy: Parents, Children, and Educators in Interaction* (2013), as a number of chapters within this volume (Schwartz, Moin, and Klayle; Moin, Protassova, Lukkari, and Schwartz; Conteh, Riasat, and Begum) specifically look at the relationship between language education and home language use. Similarly, a number of articles (Conteh, Lytra, Schwartz, and Moin) in the recent (2012) special issue of *Journal of Multilingual and Multicultural Development* on FLP also emphasise the importance of education in FLP research. These studies focus primarily on the impact of minority language education in the form of complementary education as well as bilingual provision within compulsory education. In general, the availability of minority language in a school context is seen to positively influence the child's overall minority language development, but again, the asymmetry between the minority and majority cultures is highlighted. For example, Schwartz, Moin, and Klayle (2013) find that in Arabic-Hebrew preschools in Israel, children from Arabic-speaking homes acquire Hebrew to a greater fluency than children from Hebrew-speaking homes acquire Arabic, due to the dominance of Hebrew in the wider society.

Another important direction in FLP research has been in conceptualising language use in the family within the vein of language *policy*, a framework that is usually associated with the higher echelons of social organisation. In using the framework to examine families in multilingual settings, a number of studies specifically orient to Spolsky's (2004) model of language policy (for example, King, Fogle, and Logan-Terry, 2008; Altman, Feldman, Yitzhaki, Lotem, and Walters, 2014; Chatzidaki and Maligkoudi, 2013). Fogle and King (2013, p. 1) have summarised this orientation to Spolsky (2004) as an attempt to 'to gain insights into family language ideologies (how family members think about language), language practices (what they do with language), and language management (what they try to do with language).' In particular, recent FLP work has focused on the crucial role that language *ideologies*, which, following Spolsky and Shohamy (2000), are defined using Silverstein's definition (1979, p. 93) as 'sets of beliefs about language articulated by users as a rationalisation or justification of perceived language structure or use,' play in the decision-making processes families face and in turn how these decision-making processes manifest themselves in actual language use (for example, de Houwer, 1998; Li, 1999; Yamamoto, 1995; King and Fogle, 2006; Ó hIfearnáin, 2007, 2013; Curdt-Christiansen, 2009; Kopeliovich, 2010; Kirsch, 2012). However, as King (2000) discusses, pro-minority language ideologies do not necessarily directly translate into minority language maintenance, and as also argued in Dauenhauer and Dauenhauer (1998), these pro-minority language ideologies often are in conflict with other deeply ingrained language ideologies resulting from the majority/minority asymmetry. Furthermore, as Gafaranga (2010, p. 242) emphasises and as will be demonstrated in this book, speakers are often unaware of the conversational mechanisms by which language shift is perpetuated and therefore unknowingly participate in its continuation despite their pro-minority language ideologies.

From this introduction, it is clear that FLP covers a range of foci and contexts. In looking at the three prototypical contexts – OPOL, immigrant community,[1] and autochthonous community – it is possible to postulate about the potential advantages and disadvantages of each prototype. In OPOL families, the onus to maintain the minority language tends to fall primarily on the minority language-speaking parent, usually without mainstream educational support in the minority language. However, OPOL families tend to be middle class; as well, they generally have similar, if not equal, social status vis-à-vis the dominant culture, especially since one of the parents is usually a member of the dominant culture. Further, in many cases the minority language is actually a majority language in its own right. In immigrant community contexts, by virtue of being part of a community, the child may have multiple interlocutors with whom to use the minority language, which may include family members; however, the group and their language is usually stigmatised at some wider level and there is usually no mainstream institutional educational support for the children in their minority language. In autochthonous minority communities, the child may both have multiple interlocutors, including many family members, who speak the minority language and depending on institutional support of language revitalisation, may also have access to mainstream education in the minority language. However, like immigrant communities, autochthonous communities most likely face stigmatisation at some level, and in their case, this stigmatisation may have endured for centuries and be well-ingrained in institutional contexts. It should be emphasised that these are prototypes only and are simply meant to emphasise how *context* can play an important role the likelihood of a particular

DOI: 10.1057/9781137521811.0006

FLP's success. In many cases, the boundaries between each prototype may be blurred or the realities listed as the hallmarks of each prototype may in fact not be realities at all; for example, due to reverse diasporic ideology underpinning the state of Israel, immigrants are required to learn Hebrew to participate in wider Israeli society, but they may not face the same asymmetrical social status that they would face in other nations with a clear dominant culture (for example, Russian immigrants in Israel in Kopeliovich's [2013] study versus Mexican immigrants in the United States in Bayley, Schecter, and Torres-Ayala's [1996] study). Further, due to an increasing understanding of bilingualism and multiculturalism, as well as opportunities for mobility in general, there are also potentially increasing opportunities for immigrant and OPOL children to attend complementary or compulsory education in the minority language (see for example, Conteh, 2012; Moin, Protassova, Lukkari, and Schwartz, 2013; Schwartz, Moin, and Klayle, 2013).

Despite these contextual differences and nuances, however, it is clear to see that at some level, what all FLP studies are concerned with is what Luykx (2003, p. 41) refers to as the 'language ecology of the family,' in which the fundamental question is how this ecology contributes to or detracts from the child's development and use of the minority language. However, using the term 'Family Language Policy' emphasises the *agency* that brings about a particular language ecology and how this agency is situated within a wider sociocultural framework. So often the child's language acquisition in the home is seen as a natural, organic process, one that simply 'happens,' a view which can most likely be attributed to a largely Western monolingual vantage point – after all, monolinguals living in a largely monolingual environment do not face the same decisions that multilingual families or families in multilingual environments face. FLP therefore, is the study of the role that language beliefs play in these decision-making *processes* (*cf.* Okita, 2002, p. 3); how these beliefs are situated within a wider sociocultural system; and how the beliefs and the way in which they are situated play out at the level of language practices in the family. In turn, FLP also examines how these language practices contribute to (or fail to contribute to) the child's development in the minority language. Related to Fishman's characterisation of intergenerational transmission as the 'fulcrum' in RLS, Spolsky (2012) refers to FLP as the 'critical domain' in the FLP special issue of the *Journal of Multilingual and Multicultural Development*. Clearly, FLP is central to minority language maintenance and what is at stake in this critical domain is contingent on the particular context; in OPOL situations, it is

DOI: 10.1057/9781137521811.0006

the child's maintenance of the language of one the caregivers; for the child in an immigrant situation, it can be maintenance of the heritage language in the community, and for the child in an autochthonous language community, the fate of the entire language can rest on its acquisition and use by young children.

The present study looks at the language ecology of the Campbell family, an extended family on the Isle of Skye, Scotland, where all family members have some ability in Scottish Gaelic. Using a long-term ethnographic approach as well as analyses of two corpora recorded five years apart (2009 and 2014), this study examines how the mother (Peigi) and the paternal grandmother (Nana) of the three children in the study (David, Maggie, and Jacob) try to create and maintain a Gaelic-centred FLP but how the diachronic and synchronic realities of language shift in the family means that the Gaelic-centred FLP is constantly unravelling. It also looks at how the children's wider sociocultural environment further contributes to the unravelling of the FLP. At the heart of this study is the question of why, despite the Campbell family children's apparent advantage over OPOL and immigrant community children in terms of number of minority language-speaking interlocutors *and* minority language education, the Campbell children still evidence low use of the minority language. Studies on autochthonous minority languages, as well as studies involving multi-generational extended families, are few in comparison to studies that involve situations where the 'minority' language is actually a majority language in another context or studies that focus on what is often referred to as the 'nuclear' family (see Lanza, 2007; King and Fogle, 2013). Similarly, studies of *language shift* often orient more towards the wider macro-social processes of a language's decline rather than emphasise the child's role and viewpoint in this process. This study therefore aims to contribute to filling these lacunae by taking a specifically child- and FLP-centred approach to investigating language shift, which in turn is hoped to contribute to a deeper understanding of how this process may be arrested.

Scottish Gaelic

Scottish Gaelic, henceforth simply 'Gaelic', is a Celtic language and linguistically most closely related to Irish and Manx, with the other Celtic languages – Welsh, Breton, and Cornish – forming the other branch of

DOI: 10.1057/9781137521811.0006

the Celtic language family. Gaelic was once spoken over nearly all of what is modern-day Scotland, but its decline began as early as the twelfth century with the escalating divide between the more urbanised Lowlands and the rural mountainous Highlands. The overarching socioeconomic structure of the latter region, which lacks much agricultural productivity due to the unfavourable climate and environment, has been, and still to an extent is today, that of landlord-tenant, whereby the majority of the population lived on small subsistence farm holdings called 'crofts.' Over the centuries, Gaelic began to become confined to the Highlands and especially to the islands off the west coast of Scotland known as the Hebrides. Voluntary migration from this area due to widespread poverty, as well as forced migration during the Clearances in the eighteenth and nineteenth centuries, in which landlords evicted their tenants in order to consolidate croft land into more profitable sheep grazing areas, as well as the devastating effects of two world wars, have further contributed to low population densities in the Highlands and the Hebrides (see Withers, 1984, 1988; MacKinnon, 1991 for more detailed overviews on Gaelic in Scotland). The confinement of the language primarily to this area has also resulted in the historical association of the language with poverty, rural life, and general backwardness and this low status vis-à-vis English has been further compounded by the language's stigmatisation within the education system: the 1872 Education Act made no provision for Gaelic and throughout the nineteenth and early twentieth centuries, there are accounts of children being punished for speaking the language in school (see for example, MacKinnon 1974, p. 55). Further, the practice of boarding students on the mainland or in more urbanised areas in the Hebrides, such as Portree and Stornoway, for secondary school meant that pupils from strongly Gaelic-speaking areas were forced to acculturate to the norms of places where the language shift was the most acute; in other words, they had to adopt English as their normative mode of communication. It was not until 2005 that Gaelic was given official recognition as a language of Scotland with the passing of Gaelic Language (Scotland) Act, which also set up the Gaelic language planning body *Bòrd na Gàidhlig*. Although the Gaelic Language Act's importance cannot be overlooked, it has also been criticised for vagueness and significant gaps (see Walsh and McLeod, 2007 for a full discussion of the shortcomings).

At the time that Gaelic was made an official language of Scotland, there were 58,652 speakers of Gaelic in Scotland, according to the 2001 Census. This figure indicated a sharp decline in the decrease over a ten

DOI: 10.1057/9781137521811.0006

year period, as the number of Gaelic speakers had fallen by 16.8% from the 1991 Census. This overall decline was also echoed in the heartland areas, as MacKinnon (2009, p. 589–590) points out that only 4,774 speakers (8.1%) of the total lived in areas where 70% or more spoke the language, meaning that everyday Gaelic usage had now become a minority activity in its own 'heartland' areas. However, the 2001 Census also evidenced an increase in the number of people able to read and write in Gaelic as well as an increase in the number of people aged 5–9 able to speak Gaelic (General Register Office for Scotland, 2005). The most recent Census (2011) reported 57,375 speakers, which comprises 1.1% of the population of Scotland and indicates a drop of only 2.2% from the previous Census. Like the 2001 Census, the 2011 Census also evidenced an increase of younger speakers, as the number of speakers under the age of 20 rose by .1% (National Records of Scotland, 2013; see also the analysis on Bella Caledonia, 2013). However, despite these encouraging results in terms of arresting language shift, the 2011 Census also indicates a decline in the heartland areas, with only little more than half (52%; 14,066 speakers in total) of the population of Na h-Eileanan Siar (the Western Isles), which is currently considered to be the 'core' Gaelic-speaking heartland, returned as Gaelic speakers. This decline in the heartland areas is also echoed in the findings of the Shawbost report (Munro, Taylor, and Armstrong, 2011), which used the core heartland community of Siabost on the Isle of Lewis as a case study in gauging the decline of the language. Page 4 of the report emphasises:

> The passing of Gaelic from one generation to the next – intergenerational transmission – has all but ended in Shawbost. Fluent speakers are not using Gaelic often enough in daily life in the community to ensure that Gaelic is transmitted to the younger generations, or to family and neighbours. The language is falling apart and may be dead as a community language in Shawbost within one or perhaps two generations.

Despite this rather unsettling prediction of the future of the language in a core heartland community, it is important to highlight that the last few decades have also seen considerable efforts to maintain the language. One significant development has been in the form of what was originally referred to as 'bilingual education' and has later become to be known as 'Gaelic Medium Education' (GME), in which students' subjects are taught through the medium of Gaelic. As of 2011–2012, there were a total of 2,418 pupils enrolled in GME at the primary level (0.7% of the total

DOI: 10.1057/9781137521811.0006

primary roll in Scotland) and 1,104 pupils at the secondary level (.4% of the secondary roll) (Galloway, 2012). It should be noted that with three exceptions – *Sgoil Ghàidhlig Ghlaschu* in Glasgow, *Bun-sgoil Ghàidhlig Inbhir Nis* in Inverness, and *Bun-sgoil Taobh na Pàirce* in Edinburgh – however, this immersive environment does not extend to the school as a whole, as GME classes are 'units' within wider English-speaking schools. This means that many of the students' wider experiences within the school, such as assemblies and after-school activities, are in English, which may give rise to the students feeling like a different 'tribe' from the mainstream English-speaking school, as highlighted in Morrison's (2006, p. 145) study of GME pupils in the Western Isles. Being part of a wider English school is a further contributing factor to as why, despite receiving their instruction through the medium of Gaelic, GME pupils use English as their peer group language, a reality which is also due primarily to their higher linguistic competence, and therefore greater ease, in using English, as a number of GME pupils do not come from homes where Gaelic is used (O' Hanlon, McLeod, and Paterson, 2010, p. 44). Thus, while GME has the potential to play a vital role in the revitalisation of the language, there are many challenges with bringing this potential to fruition, not least of which is also the continuity of leaving school and then subsequently using Gaelic as an adult, as shown in Dunmore's (2015) recent PhD thesis on the linguistic experiences of adults who attended GME in the 1980s–1990s.

Another revitalisation effort has been in Gaelic media. With the inception of *Radio nan Gàidheal* in 1985 and then its expansion in 1996, Gaelic radio has grown over the last three decades and is currently available on broadcast radio as well as live streaming and catch-up services on the Internet. In 2008, the Gaelic television station *BBC Alba* was launched but it did not become available on all delivery platforms until 2011. One continuing challenge apart from the fact that both these services are publically funded in a time of economic downturn is the issue of human resources. With less than 58,000 speakers, the pool to draw from in finding Gaelic speakers for the appropriate broadcast roles is much smaller than in English language media; however; the converse to this disadvantage is that it allows people who normally would never be on mainstream radio or TV to have this opportunity. This may be particularly advantageous in encouraging children to use the language through participation in the media and through forming a positive image of the language, both concepts of which are encapsulated in FilmG, a Gaelic

DOI: 10.1057/9781137521811.0006

short film contest aimed at school-aged children. However, another problem associated with Gaelic media, as noted in Cormack (1993), is how early broadcasting in particular catered primarily to the ageing sector of the population. Although more recent Gaelic programming has tried to reach a more diverse audience in terms of age demographics, a recent report commissioned by BBC Alba revealed that adolescents tend to think of BBC Alba as aimed either at their grandparents' generation or at very young children (Graffman, 2014).

There are many more Gaelic revitalisation issues that could be discussed here; however, as the aim of this book is to discuss Gaelic language shift from a child-centred point of view, only the most relevant points in terms of the children's immediate sociocultural environment were chosen for elaboration. It should be emphasised, however, that in spite of the language revitalisation efforts, Gaelic has a clear minority status within the UK, Scotland, and as shown by the most recent Census results as well as the Shawbost study, also within the traditional heartland areas. In many ways, this book is about how one family is trying to swim against the tide of the seemingly impossible force of belonging to a minority culture that speaks a highly endangered language.

Gaelic on Skye

The Isle of Skye (*An t-Eilean Sgitheanach* in Gaelic) is Scotland's second largest island, covering an area of 645.8 square miles (167,261.18 hectares) and is connected to the mainland by a bridge opened in 1995. In the 1881 Census, the entire population of the island was reported as Gaelic-speaking, with one-third of the population of the northwest part of the island and one-quarter of the more urbanised southeast part returned as monoglot Gaelic speakers. However, this changed over the course of the next century, with only 67.2% of the population reported as Gaelic speakers in 1981 in the northwest and 49.4% in the southeast (Duwe, 2006a, b). This shift over a century was precipitated by a rapid decline in intergenerational transmission as documented by the Scottish Council for Research on Education in 1961. Of pupils in the first two years of primary school (aged 5–7) in Skye, nearly half of those returned as 'English first language' (53 out of 125) had Gaelic-speaking parents, meaning that parents were choosing to raise their children as English speakers. By the 1970s, English was firmly established as the peer group language for children entering school during this decade and afterwards (Smith-Christmas and Smakman, 2009).

DOI: 10.1057/9781137521811.0006

This generational lacuna has resulted in a low proportion of Gaelic speakers on Skye in the present day: of a total population of 9,710 people aged 3 and over, 2,865 (29.4%) reported in the last Census (2011) that they could speak Gaelic. A further approximate 6.6% of the population identified themselves as passive bilinguals. With less than half of the population being able to even understand Gaelic, it is clear to see that for the most part, Gaelic cannot be used as a community language in Skye. Home generational transmission remains low as well: 1,684 people (17.3%) reported Gaelic as the language that they used at home, while 7,730 people (78.6%) of the population reported using only English at home. In many cases, use of Gaelic at home may well not mean that Gaelic is the exclusive or dominant language of the home, but rather, that *some* Gaelic is used in the home.

Despite the decline of Gaelic on Skye, it is important to note that certain maintenance developments, particularly in terms of education, have been made in recent years. Bilingual education began in Skye in 1978 and by 1985, all primary schools in Skye had bilingual provision (MacKinnon, 1991; Robertson, 2003). Currently, there are 91 nursery pupils and 244 primary pupils enrolled in GME on Skye; further, 121 secondary pupils are taking subjects taught through the medium of Gaelic (Highland Council website, 2015; see also Müller, 2006 for more on secondary GME provision in Skye). The building of a dedicated GME primary school is also underway in Portree, the main urban centre on the island. The other main educational development on Skye has been the founding of the Gaelic medium college Sabhal Mòr Ostaig, located in Sleat on the southeast of the island, in 1973. Sabhal Mòr Ostaig is one of the main institutional bulwarks of Gaelic language maintenance, not only in its role in the learning and teaching of the language to adults, but in its ideological stance and reification of a *Gàidhlig a-mhàin* (Gaelic only) policy. However, it should be emphasised that just as Gaelic's status as a minority language is a striking reality on a national level despite various revitalisation efforts, so too is this the case in Skye as a whole.

Summary

In tracing FLP research from its inception in the early twentieth century through to present day studies, this chapter has delineated three proto-types of FLP research: the OPOL context, the immigrant community

DOI: 10.1057/9781137521811.0006

context, and the autochthonous minority language community context. The chapter has argued that what connects these different contexts and foci under the umbrella of FLP research is that they are all centred on the key question of why some children acquire and use more of the minority language than others; and that in investigating this question, researchers use the child's experiences in the family as the locus of analysis. The chapter has also emphasised that studies of autochthonous minority languages, as well as studies that involve extended families, are few in comparison to other contexts. The chapter concluded by giving a brief overview of how the autochthonous minority language under investigation in this study, Scottish Gaelic, has undergone severe shift and the chapter further discussed how despite this shift, there have also been significant revitalisation efforts made on behalf of the language in recent years.

Note

1   Although Yates and Terraschke's study (2013) involves immigrants who speak languages that are not the majority language in the home country, to the best of my knowledge there is no FLP study that specifically looks at the context of autochthonous minority language speakers who then have immigrated to a new country.

DOI: 10.1057/9781137521811.0006

2
Methodology

Abstract: *The present FLP study is primarily centred on an eight-year ethnography of the Campbell family and microinteractional analyses of two corpora of their naturally occurring interactions, recorded in 2009 and 2014. The overall ethnography of the family has been largely shaped by my different interests in their language use, which have shifted over the years due to various different projects. As these shifts in focus have been instrumental in how I analyse the Campbells' FLP for the current project, I will present the methodological account in a chronological format. In doing so, I hope to elucidate the decisions made and challenges overcome looking at how this family's FLP has changed over time.*

Keywords: ethnography; spontaneous speech; transcriptions

Smith-Christmas, Cassie. *Family Language Policy: Maintaining an Endangered Language in the Home.* Basingstoke: Palgrave Macmillan, 2016. DOI: 10.1057/9781137521811.0007.

DOI: 10.1057/9781137521811.0007

Beginning an eight-year ethnography

As can be gleaned from the introductory chapter, the diverse foci of FLP has resulted in a range of methodological approaches. In some cases, the researcher is also the parent of the child and these studies centre on observations and sometimes recordings of the child's language use as it unfolds in everyday actions, as well as the parent–researcher's reflections on his or her own language use with the child (for example, Ronjat, 1913; Leopold, 1939–1949; Fantini, 1985; Kopeliovich, 2013). Studies where the researcher is not the child's parent, such as de Houwer (1990) and Lanza (1997), also use these methods, employing prearranged observation sessions with the family as well as recordings of caregiver–child interactions. The more recent focus on language ideologies has resulted in a number of studies using interviews with caregivers (for example, Kirsch, 2012) or surveys about language use (for example, Schwartz, 2008; Ó hIfearnain, 2013) as the primary locus of the analysis. Studies of immigrant or autochthonous minority communities often centre on ethnographic methodologies, especially that of participant observation, whereby the researcher experiences social life along with the speakers, in examining FLP from a more community-centred framework (for example, Kulick, 1992; Li Wei, 1994). Many FLP studies combine a variety of techniques (interviews, recordings, participant observation), as exemplified for instance in Curdt-Christiansen's (2009) study of the FLPs of Chinese families in Montreal, in which she combined interviews with weekly visits, recordings, and overall participation in the community

This study also uses a variety of methodological approaches in coming to an understanding of the Campbell family's FLP over time. The journey first began in March 2007, when at the encouragement of my MA supervisor Dick Smakman at the University of Leiden in the Netherlands, I undertook a study of the linguistic components of language shift over three generations of a language that I did not yet speak. This initial difficulty was largely mitigated through the assistance of eminent Gaelic sociolinguist Nancy Dorian, who kindly typed up and shared her test sentences used for her 1974 and 1976 studies of East Sutherland Gaelic. The next challenge was finding three generations of a Gaelic-speaking family willing to participate in the study I had designed. I wrote a letter to the editor of the *West Highland Free Press*, one of the newspapers that serves areas where Gaelic is still spoken, and I was very fortunate when my letter was answered by Nana, who invited me to stay with her family

DOI: 10.1057/9781137521811.0007

for as long as I liked. In other research, one might be wary of speakers who seem overly eager to participate in a study, as enthusiastic participants may not be representative of a 'typical' speaker in a particular community (see for example, Eckert, 1989); however, as gleaned from the introduction, the very nature of what I was trying to ascertain necessitated that in many ways, the family I studied must be *atypical*, as attempting to maintain Gaelic in the family is going against the grains of community norms not only on Skye, but Scotland as a whole, including areas which are considered Gaelic-speaking 'heartlands' (*cf.* the Shawbost report [Munro, Taylor, and Armstrong, 2011]).

I initially stayed with Nana in her house on the Isle of Skye for ten days. During these ten days, I was warmly welcomed by the whole family and my status in many ways quickly changed from 'researcher' to 'friend of the family.' I was able to conduct my MA thesis, which confirmed language shift from a linguistic point of view as well as a social perspective (see Smakman and Smith-Christmas, 2008; Smith-Christmas and Smakman, 2009). Crucially, this visit lay the groundwork for my understanding of the sociological factors underpinning the rapid language shift from Nana's generation to her own children's generation. What intrigued me most about the family was the fact that although there appeared to be a generational lacuna of Gaelic use, it was clear that as a whole, the family was trying to maintain Gaelic with the third generation, which at that time consisted of David (4;7) and Maggie (1;0). It was also clear that David was an active Gaelic user and despite his young age, he received the highest score on the linguistic component of the study when compared to his third generational cohort.[1]

After the initial visit, I made two more visits to the family in 2007, once in May and once in July. These visits compounded my understanding of the extent to which the Campbell family were going against the grains of community norms by trying to raise the third generation as Gaelic speakers. In May 2007, for example, while on a ferry to another, more strongly Gaelic-speaking Hebridean island, a man came up to Nana and praised her for her use of Gaelic with David, remarking on how unusual it was for people to speak to children in Gaelic. In September of that same year, I moved to the US, and thus I maintained my relationship with the Campbell family via e-mail correspondence and occasional Skype and telephone calls. Over the course of this year, Nana relayed to me how Maggie spoke far less Gaelic than David had at that age. I saw the truth in Nana's statement for myself upon my next visit to the family in

DOI: 10.1057/9781137521811.0007

October 2008, which was shortly after I began my PhD at the University of Glasgow. What was most striking to me was that in just over the course of this year, David had gone from being a high user of Gaelic to a low user of the language. As well, David's Gaelic sounded considerably more Anglified than it had in 2007. Various family members also remarked on David's Gaelic, both on use and content, confirming my hypotheses that not only was David using much less Gaelic than he had at 4;7 but also that his Gaelic was becoming increasingly influenced by English.

Since 2008, I have visited the family every few months and usually average a minimum of five visits per year. While visiting with Nana and her family, I simply participate and observe life as it unfolds in the Campbell family. I eat with the family; play with the children; help with household chores; visit other relatives and friends with them; go shopping; go out for meals and occasionally accompany the second generation members on work excursions or social outings. In short, I live life how the Campbell family members live it as much as I can when I am there. I also have ample opportunities to ask them about their language use, both past and present, as well as their language beliefs and their perceptions of Gaelic use in the community. As the family knows that I am interested in their language use, they often explicitly discuss these topics while I am visiting.

Apart from when I stayed on Harris with the family, during these visits, I always stay in Nana's house. In Milroy's (1987) celebrated account of working-class Belfast neighbourhoods, she observes how people simply walk into each other's houses without knocking. No description could be truer of anything than it is of Nana's house. Two of Nana's siblings and also Nana's three children live within a 20-minute drive of Nana's house. Each day, usually at least one of Nana's children and one of her siblings is at her house for a meal or a visit. Crucially for conducting a study on FLP, Nana's grandchildren live on the same croft land as Nana. Their house is located approximately 100 metres behind Nana's own house, which means that the grandchildren have the freedom to move between both houses. It is not uncommon for Nana to receive a phone call from the children's house asking if a particular child is there, as if the child is not in his or her own house, he or she is assumed to be at Nana's. Nana frequently looks after the children, particularly when the children's parents are both working. Other family members often present in Nana's house (Nana's sister, Nana's own children) also usually assume caregiver roles vis-à-vis the children. If she has not seen her grandchildren during the day, Nana will usually go up to their house for a visit. Thus, by staying with Nana, I have access to observing multiple family members' interactions with each other and most importantly, their interactions with the youngest members of the Campbell family.

Recording, transcribing, and analysing spontaneous speech: the 2009 corpus

In 2009, I recorded the Campbell family's naturally occurring, spontaneously spoken interactions for my PhD thesis, which was centred on the differences in their generational language practices and in particular, on their use of code-switching, which in this case refers to their alternating use of Gaelic and English. For this study, I included not only the Campbell family members involved in this current FLP study, but also Nana's extended family on both the Isles of Skye and Harris. I approached this study of code-switching from a microinteractional framework, which uses the fine-grained mechanics of conversation (including for example repairs, pauses, and repetitions) to arrive at an understanding of why speakers make various code choices over the course of a particular interaction and how these choices are related to wider sociocultural norms and beliefs about language use. I therefore situated the generational language practices of the Campbell family within a field of inquiry pioneered by Auer (1984, 1988) and successfully applied to analysing family and/or interactions with children both within Auer's own work as well as the work of Li Wei (1994, 1998), Cromdal (2001, 2004, 2005) and Gafaranga (2010, 2011), among others. Situating myself within this framework provided the motivation for recording the family's everyday interactions over a two-week period in July 2009. In April 2009, while I was in Skye for an immersion Gaelic course at Sabhal Mòr Ostaig, I piloted recording the family over the weekends. This pilot proved fruitful in many ways, as I realised that although I had originally planned to leave the recording device with Nana and simply allow her to record at her discretion, it would be more advantageous if I were to use a participant observation approach to record the family's interactions. Not only did I worry that Nana might forget to turn the recording device on and might become stressed in the running and maintenance of the equipment (especially sending/transferring files), but I realised that I would have a much better understanding of the conversations, and

DOI: 10.1057/9781137521811.0007

therefore a more accurate interpretation for analysis, if I were present. It was therefore arranged that I would come and stay with the family for two weeks in July 2009 and record as many interactions as I could.

The process of recording anyone's interactions, let alone a family's private interactions, entails a number of ethical and theoretical issues. Prior to the April 2009 recordings, I was required to apply for ethical clearance from the University of Glasgow. Speakers therefore signed consent forms stating that they knew that they were being recorded, that they understood what the recordings were being used for, and that they knew that they could have the recording device turned off at any point and any part they wished deleted. Participants rarely exercised these latter rights, but they did surface occasionally. Additionally, I would sometimes pre-emptively turn off the recording device if I thought they were talking about a particularly sensitive issue, such as business-related matters or if the children were being unusually badly behaved. The children sometimes asked me to turn the recording device off, but this appeared to be more a reflex of the fact that they felt they had power over me by telling me what to do and the fact that I had to do what they said, rather than the fact that they did not want to be recorded at a particular moment. I had the children listen back to parts of the recordings so they could understand what I was doing. They quickly grew used to me recording and even referred to my recording device as my 'teddy bear' because I always had it with me.

The main theoretical issue in recording a corpus of natural, spontaneous speech is the Observer's Paradox: to what extent did the fact that the family knew they were being recorded influence their linguistic behaviour? In general, a number of key aspects of my relationship with the family and the recording process mean that I believe the recording excerpts used for analysis in this book accurately represent the family's normal use of language. The fact that I had been observing the family's language use prior to recording them meant that I was able to discard any recordings that I felt did not reflect their actual language practices. This was the case, for example, when Nana's sister had not been recorded for a few days and used nearly monolingual Gaelic in a particular recording, which is highly unusual for her. I therefore did not transcribe or include this recording in the corpus. Further, Labov (1970) notes that recording family members interacting with each other is conducive to obtaining natural, vernacular speech, as the fact that they are speaking to people they know very well minimises the presence of the researcher

DOI: 10.1057/9781137521811.0007

and the recording device. This appeared to be the case with the Campbell family recordings and it is evident in some of the recordings that family members forgot that they were being recorded. For example, in one interaction between Nana and her cousin, I left the room and Nana started talking about me. She then began to laugh, as she realised that I would of course be listening to the recording later. I also think the fact that at this point in time the family was used to thinking of me as a 'non-Gaelic speaker' also contributed to speakers' (especially Nana's) use of natural speech, as they were somewhat used to being able to say things around me that they knew I would not understand.

Although having limited abilities in the language may have been advantageous during the recording process, it naturally proved problematic when I later had to transcribe the corpus. In general, instances where the caregivers were speaking directly to the children were easier to understand, as these utterances tend to be simpler and employ less code-switching. This is not to say that recordings involving the children were necessarily easy; child language can be very difficult to understand, not only from a productive point of view, but also from a practical point of view, as in many recordings, the children are much more mobile than the adults and therefore frequently move away from the recording device. Further, sometimes the children's singing, crying, and general 'noise' presents a further challenge in transcribing what adults are saying. The majority of the conversations between the first generation members were also particularly difficult, as not only is the main interlocutor (Nana) a very fast talker, but the issue of code-switching and frequent repairs meant that the limits for interpretation are broader, which sometimes led to some laughable transcriptions on my part. For example, near the end of a particularly long and complicated narrative (see Smith-Christmas, 2012) I mistakenly transcribed *bhri- ghoirt* ('brea(k)- hurt') as a nonsensical onomatopoeic 'fish fush', as either Gaelic or English was equally likely and Nana often uses onomatopoeic sounds in her speech. However, this issue and multiple others were cleared up when I spent two weeks in 2010 with Nana verifying my transcriptions. Aside from sometimes being tedious and extremely time-consuming, it was also amusing (Nana howled when she saw 'fish fush' in the transcription) and the verification process allowed me to make more sense of the first generation conversations, as it was only after Nana re-told me the long narrative with 'fish fush' was I able to fully make sense of the story as a whole.

DOI: 10.1057/9781137521811.0007

As will become evident in the transcriptions both in Gaelic and English, natural speech is a messy process and speakers are liable to make a number of 'mistakes' when speaking either language, irrespective of their linguistic competence. Great care was taken to transcribe speech as it was *actually said*, including multiple repairs and reformulations such as the one just discussed. Nana was sometimes tempted to 'correct' her speech in the transcription process; further, because of my own Gaelic proficiency, I sometimes would look up words that I did not know and therefore would be tempted to transcribe words/phrases in their canonical 'correct' forms, such as basing a word or phrase on the dictionary-given gender of a noun for example, instead of transcribing it as I heard it. However, both Nana and I suppressed these tendencies as best we could so that the transcriptions reflect natural communication as it occurs, not how people think it *should* occur. This was important not only for the purposes of analysis, but as there are few corpora of spontaneous Gaelic-English speech, it was very important that I have a record of possible language change in progress. Occasionally, orthography was modified to represent various dialectal (and occasionally possibly some idiolectal) features that speakers use, such as Nana's addition of an alveolar stop in the verbal noun *a' smaoineachadh* ('thinking'), as she often says it as *smaointeachadh* or part of a word or phrase may be put in parentheses if the sound was not heard but the word/phrase would look too strange without it.

During the transcription process, the issue of anonymity also became very important. 'Campbell' is a pseudonym and all speakers have been given pseudonyms for their first names. First name pseudonyms in the Campbell family are matched with their real names for possibility of lenition, which would occur in some cases but not others if speakers are addressing each other using the vocative (for example the name Màiri becomes Mhàiri in the vocative. The 'mh' equates to a nasalised [v]). Any person that family members refer to who is not part of the family is also given a pseudonym. As Skye is a relatively small and close-knit community, both on the island itself and among those who have left the island, particularly those who have settled in Glasgow, it would be possible that if I were to impart certain details about the family, people would easily be able to work out who the Campbells are. For this reason, I have been intentionally vague in disclosing certain details about the family, such as where they live or their occupations. However, even in withholding a number of details, I have not been entirely successful in

DOI: 10.1057/9781137521811.0007

keeping them truly anonymous, as various people have seen me out with the family when I am in Skye. This is an unavoidable part of my research, but bearing this anonymity issue in mind, I have always taken care in my research not to show conversational examples that may be particularly embarrassing for them. This is particularly relevant in the case of the children in the study; although they were aware they were being recorded at the time, I am cognizant of the fact that when they grow older, they might be particularly embarrassed by certain excerpts and I therefore exercise caution when deciding which excerpts to show in my research.

From the verification process emerged ten hours of data that I used for analysis. Besides analysing excerpts from conversations using a microinteractional approach, I also looked at the Campbells' use of language use from a quantitative perspective. For this task, I chose the conversational turn as the unit of measurement. Although this is not without its inherent problems, the main one being that a turn can range from a single word to near-soliloquies, this was deemed the best way to arrive at an overall picture of language choice in the Campbell family. Turns were coded as monolingual Gaelic if the entire turn was in Gaelic; English if the turn was monolingual English; Mixed if the turn included code-switching and/or borrowing; and Undecided for difficult cases. These difficult cases were mainly instances where a speaker (generally a first generation speaker, in particular, Nana) would use an English word in an otherwise Gaelic utterance; because of the high integration and proliferation of English words in Gaelic, it sometimes gave a disingenuous picture of language choice if the utterances were coded as 'Mixed', especially when taking the speakers', not the linguists', point of view of code choice (*cf.* Meeuwis and Blommaert, 1998). From the coding process emerged a total of 5015 turns.

This qualitative and quantitative analysis eventually took the form of my PhD thesis, which was completed in 2012. In writing up my PhD, I continued to visit the Campbell family regularly and keep in touch via e-mail, phone, and increasingly over Facebook. I have given them copies of all my work, including my PhD thesis and they have often enjoyed looking at the conversational extracts and laughing over things they said years ago. In 2012, I took up a Soillse fellowship for the University of the Highlands and Islands on the Isle of Lewis and over the course of this fellowship, have continued regular visits and contact with the Campbell family as well as recruited them for participation in a number of other

DOI: 10.1057/9781137521811.0007

projects. These have included a project led by Maria Parafita-Couto in looking at the grammatical aspects of Gaelic-English code-switching, a project about migration to the Highlands and Islands, and, most importantly in terms of this current study, an ethnographic project commissioned by BBC Alba, where, among other tasks, I spent eight to ten hours observing the children's use of media in the home.

Recording, transcribing, and analysing spontaneous speech: the 2014 corpus

I am clearly very lucky to have found such a kind and patient family in accommodating my research interests and in 2014, I decided to try their patience once more by recording another corpus similar to the 2009 corpus. The reason underlying this decision was that although by this time I had written a thesis and several other papers on their language practices, I still had not come to a full conclusion as to why, despite having multiple minority language interlocutors *and* minority language immersion education, the third generation (David, Maggie, and by this time, Jacob) did not evidence much Gaelic use. I therefore recorded another corpus of the family's interactions in July 2014, by which time another child (Jacob) had been born and another one was on the way. Unlike the 2009 corpus, which included the extended family living both in Harris and Skye, the shift in focus to FLP meant that I decided to only record interactions among the Skye Campbells who interact with the third generation on a regular basis.[2] However, aside from this streamlining of focus in terms of speakers, and the fact that I now applied for ethical approval with the University of the Highlands and Islands instead of the University of Glasgow, the aim of the 2014 recordings was to as closely as possible replicate the 2009 corpus. To a large extent, this was achieved, as I recorded the speakers in a variety of daily life situations. However, as the recording is situated in on how life unfolds naturally in the family, certain changes, mostly relating to speakers' occupations, resulted in differences in the corpora. For example, the 2009 corpus includes a number of recordings of the children's father interacting with them; however, as he now works on the mainland during the week, he was only home for one recording session. Similarly, the 2009 corpus includes a number of interactions between the children and their uncle; like the children's father, their uncle also now often works on the mainland and therefore was only recorded in an interaction with other adults. As well, because of the family's busy schedule, I was only able to record one week instead of two, meaning that the 2014 corpus is smaller (approximately six hours). Despite these differences, however, I feel that on the whole the July 2014 corpus is representative of how FLP currently plays out in the Campbell family. I also then visited the family in December of the same year and obtained approximately three hours of recordings both of spontaneous interactions as well as interviews with various family members about how they felt that language use had changed over time. Because the interview recordings were qualitatively different from the July 2009 and 2014 corpora, it was decided that only the July corpora would be used for coding analysis; however, excerpts from the December recordings will be discussed throughout the book.

In terms of the Observer's Paradox, I feel that although it was still an issue, the fact that the family had been recorded before and had sometimes intermittently been recorded in the intervening years meant that they were equally, if not more comfortable, than they had been in the 2009 recordings. The main issue with the Observer's Paradox was that some speakers had read some of my work and therefore tried to change their language practices to what they thought they *should* do. This, for example, accounts in part for the children's aunt Màiri's high degree of Gaelic in the 2014 recordings, as she was familiar with my 2014a article postulating that her use of English contributes to 'modelling' language shift to the third generation. In many ways, Màiri's Gaelic use in the 2014 corpus is reminiscent of her brother Seumas' Gaelic use in the 2009 corpus, which, as also described in the 2014a article, is postulated to be a reflex of an 'awakening' of his latent pro-Gaelic ideologies. Thus, although this Gaelic language use may not be *completely* representative of speakers' 'natural' use, the Observer's Paradox has brought language ideologies to the forefront of family interactions, which, as will be seen in the following chapters, becomes very useful in examining the relationship between ideologies and linguistic practices. Further, as will be seen throughout the excerpts in this book, the children's reactions to speakers' breaking of particular norms, such as Màiri's unusually high use of Gaelic, serve to illustrate just how entrenched certain norms are within the family.

I transcribed some of the interactions, which was much easier than in the 2009 recordings, as not only had my Gaelic improved, but I was much more familiar with the family's particular way of speaking with each other. However, as I had a grant from the Soillse Small Research Fund for the project 'Còig Bliadhna às Dèidh: A Longitudinal Study of Family Language Policy in a Gaelic-English Bilingual Family' which included transcription costs, the majority of the corpus was transcribed by my personal friend and colleague Stuart Dunmore. Because of the highly personal nature of the recordings, it naturally was important that the corpus was transcribed by someone I trusted completely. It was also important that I had someone who was experienced in transcribing spontaneous Gaelic-English speech and who understood the importance of transcribing what was *actually* said, as well as someone who had familiarity with CA conventions such as marking pauses and so forth. Although Stuart's Gaelic was more fluent than mine had been for the 2009 transcriptions, he also came up against the same various challenges I did in the 2009 transcriptions, which was made all the more difficult by the fact that he was not present for the interactions nor was he personally familiar with the family. However, by this time my own familiarity with the family and their language use, as well as the fact that I had been present in the interactions, meant that I was able to solve most of the transcription issues on my own rather than having Nana check through the transcriptions. In places of uncertainty, I have asked Nana to check the transcriptions, most recently during a visit in March 2015. Throughout the transcription process, Stuart and I met and communicated regularly about any issues that arose. It was very interesting to have someone else's insight on some of the more intriguing linguistic aspects of the corpus and checking Stuart's transcriptions helped me to realise just how idiolectal some features of the Campbell's speech may be. The 2014 Corpus was also coded according to the same criteria as the 2009 Corpus, which resulted in 2,824 turns. I coded the corpus myself and tried as best as I could to align with the choices I made in 2009, but the fact that five years had elapsed, during which time my understanding of language choice in the Campbell family has evolved, cannot go ignored. However, for both the 2009 and 2014 corpora, the coding is intended only to provide a supplementary picture of language use. The main analyses lies in the ethnographic observations as well as the microinteractional analysis of conversational extracts I deem most representative of these observations.

It goes without saying that I have been very fortunate in finding the Campbell family and for their continued kindness towards me. We have witnessed many important events in each other's lives, both happy and

DOI: 10.1057/9781137521811.0007

some unfortunately tragic, and the analysis in this book is as much about my evolving relationship with them as it is an analysis of their language practices from a research point of view. This is their story, of how they are trying to maintain a language that so many people (including some of them) have chosen to give up, and the reason why this maintenance is a continual uphill struggle.

Notes

1   In order to have as many participants as possible for my MA study, I included Nana's late husband's side of the family who live in the same village as Nana. Maggie was not included in my MA thesis because of her age.

2   For the sake of consistency, I did however include Nana's own turns when speaking to other first generation peers (Nana's cousins, her older sister and her brother) on the phone, as these accounted for a large proportion of Nana's Gaelic use in the 2009 corpus.

DOI: 10.1057/9781137521811.0007

3

A Diachronic View of FLP

Abstract: *This chapter provides an overall picture of how language use and FLP have changed in the Campbell family over time. The chapter details each speaker's social and linguistic backgrounds and demonstrates how the creation and subsequent unravelling of the current Gaelic-centred FLP (the FLP involving David, Maggie, and Jacob) is the result of different FLPs (the FLPs that the children's caregivers experienced when they were younger) and how these FLPs have converged and changed over time. The chapter underscores several observations about diachronic language use over three generations: first, that language shift is occurring along the generational dimension; secondly, language shift appears also to occur* within *generations in terms of age; and finally that the overall use of Gaelic has decreased over the two corpora.*

Keywords: language ideologies; language maintenance; language shift

Smith-Christmas, Cassie. *Family Language Policy: Maintaining an Endangered Language in the Home.* Basingstoke: Palgrave Macmillan, 2016. DOI: 10.1057/9781137521811.0008.

A quantitative view of language use over time

The following table gives the results of the coding of the two corpora as well as pertinent biographical information about each speaker. Speakers' use of each language is given in numerical totals as well as the percentage that this numerical total comprises. Although the percentages are not an absolute way to compare each speaker's language use over time, due to the issue mentioned in the last chapter of less recording time for the 2014 corpus, the percentages provide a better comparison for language use over time than do the numerical totals.

TABLE 3.1 *Overall language use in the Campbell family*

Speaker	Birth year	Sex	Relationship to third generation	Corpus	Gaelic	English	Mixed	Undecided	Total
First generation									
Nana	1946	F	Paternal grandmother		1,342 (65%)	303 (15%)	326 (16%)	88 (4%)	
				2009					2,059
				2014	598 (57%)	267 (25%)	150 (14%)	33 (3%)	1,048
Dolina	1951	F	Maternal grandmother		49 (64%)	20 (26%)	6 (8%)	2 (3%)	
				2009					77
				2014	104 (83%)	5 (4%)	13 (10%)	4 (3%)	126
Isabel	1955	F	Paternal great aunt		172 (39%)	215 (48%)	44 (10%)	15 (3%)	
				2009					446
				2014	53 (20%)	182 (69%)	28 (10%)	1 (0.4%)	264
Total					2,318 (58%)	992 (25%)	567 (14%)	143 (4%)	4,020
Second generation									
Seumas	1971	M	Paternal uncle		39 (20%)	157 (80%)	3 (2%)	0 (0%)	
				2009					199
				2014	1 (0.8%)	124 (98%)	1 (.8%)	1 (.8%)	127
Màiri	1975	F	Paternal aunt		1 (1%)	97 (98%)	0 (0%)	1 (1%)	
				2009					99
				2014	44 (19%)	177 (78%)	5 (2%)	1 (0.4%)	227
Aonghas	1978	M	Father		16 (11%)	125 (84%)	6 (4%)	2 (1%)	
				2009					149
				2014	1 (7%)	13 (93%)	0 0%	0 0%	14

(Continued)

DOI: 10.1057/1057/9781137521811.0008

TABLE 3.1 *Continued*

Speaker	Birth year	Sex	Relationship to third generation	Corpus	Gaelic	English	Mixed	Undecided	Total
	1978	F	Mother		265	35	23	30	
Peigi				2009	(75%)	(10%)	(7%)	(9%)	353
					174	63	11	7	
				2014	(68%)	(25%)	(4%)	(3%)	255
					541	791	49	42	
Total					(38%)	(56%)	(3%)	(3%)	1,423
Third generation									
	2002	M			5	191	5	0	
David				2009	(2%)	(95%)	(2%)	(%)	201
					2	152	0	0	
				2014	(1%)	(99%)	(0%)	(0%)	154
	2006	F			75	542	57	6	
Maggie				2009	(11%)	(80%)	(8%)	(.8%)	680
					15	247	14	0	
				2014	(5%)	(89%)	(5%)	(0%)	276
	2010	M			12	307	12	2	
Jacob				2014	(4%)	(92%)	(4%)	(.6%)	333
					109	1,439	88	8	
Total					(7%)	(88%)	(5%)	(.5%)	1,644
					2,968	3,222	704	193	
Total					(42%)	(45%)	(10%)	(3%)	7,087

In the December 2014 interview where I asked Nana, Isabel, and Seumas to reflect on how the family's language use had changed over seven years, at one point Nana said *tha: tha Gàidhlig a' ruith a-mach a's an teaghlach seo* ('Gaelic is running out of this family') and her sister Isabel added *am broinn an taighe* ('[from] within the house'). These two characterisations of how Gaelic use has declined in the family appear to be corroborated by the results of the quantitative component of the study, as the majority of speakers use less Gaelic than they did five years ago. Further, Gaelic decreases with each generation, culminating with the third generation only averaging 7% Gaelic use over both corpora. Even within the first generation, who are theoretically hypothesised to be the most frequent users of the language, overall Gaelic use is just above half (58%) over both corpora and in the 2014 corpus, the youngest speaker (Isabel) only evidences 20% use of the language. Overall, it appears that the family uses roughly equal Gaelic and English, but it should be emphasised that when looking at the numbers and percentages in greater detail, this reality is borne primarily out of three (Nana, Dolina, and Peigi)

DOI: 10.1057/1057/9781137521811.0008

of the ten speakers' language use. However, despite these observations of the overall decline of Gaelic in the family, it is also clear that two speakers do in fact appear to use more Gaelic in the 2014 corpus than they did in the 2009 corpus. One of these speakers is Dolina. In the 2014 corpus, Dolina is recorded in an interaction involving Nana, Peigi, the grandchildren and I, while in a similar interaction in the 2009 corpus, Nana is not present. It is hypothesised that Dolina's higher use of Gaelic may be attributed to the fact that she is interacting with a first-generation peer, which supports the premise discussed later in this chapter that the use of Gaelic between Dolina and her daughter Peigi may take more conscious effort, as both speakers are reversing years of habitual English use together, while interacting in Gaelic with a first-generation peer such as Nana is the result of normative and more unconscious Gaelic use. The other speaker whose Gaelic use increased over the span of the corpora is Màiri. As discussed in the Methodology, Màiri's increase in Gaelic is hypothesised to be related in part to her understanding of her role in perpetuating language shift in the family. This, as well as more detailed information on each speaker in the study, will be explained in the following sections.

First generation

Nana

The story of FLP in the Campbell family in many ways begins with Nana, who is the second eldest of four siblings born to two Gaelic-speaking parents from the neighbouring (and more strongly Gaelic-speaking) Isle of Harris. Nana was born on Harris, but moved to a village on the Isle of Skye as an infant. Nana reports that Gaelic was the language used in her home while growing up, both as the language used in parent-child interactions as well as amongst her siblings. It was also the language of Nana's extended family and to some extent, the language she used with friends at school, although Nana's education was in English and a number of her peers in her village were monoglot English speakers due to the ongoing language shift. Upon attending secondary school in Portree, however, English became Nana's peer group language, as Nana recalls being called 'country yokels' by the Portree adolescents for using Gaelic. Nana left Skye after secondary school to complete a degree in education at one of the large mainland universities and even though the university was located in a strongly English-speaking environment, Nana maintained the use of

DOI: 10.1057/1057/9781137521811.0008

Gaelic socially. She roomed with a Gaelic speaker and also maintained a network of Gaelic-speaking friends while at university. After university, Nana married her husband, another Gaelic speaker from Skye and shortly after their first son (Seumas) was born, the couple moved back to Skye and lived in Nana's husband's village, which is where Nana currently resides today. The couple had two more children (Màiri and Aonghas) and Nana reports that she and her husband used Gaelic with all their children.

Nana has described her and her husband's use of Gaelic to their children as 'natural,' emphasising that although Nana and her husband spoke English equally well, Gaelic felt like their native language more so than English. It was still by and large the language they used with their own parents, siblings, and other family members as well as the language they used with many community members in Skye. Nana recalls that there was 'no question' about what language the couple were going to use with their children; it was simply going to be Gaelic. Although Nana has often said to me that she has been sad at seeing her children grow up English-dominant, none of the Campbell family members remember Nana actively sanctioning their use of English. Seumas and Màiri, however, do remember how their father would sometimes grow angry when they answered him in English. Màiri also remembers how her father was very disappointed in Màiri's decision to take a major European language as a subject at school instead of Gaelic. It is clear to see that Nana and her husband set up a Gaelic-centred FLP with their own family but that from collective family memory, it was Nana's husband, not Nana, who appeared to be the main enforcer of this Gaelic-centred FLP. Nana's husband was Nana's senior by more than a decade and the family recalls how he had a deep attachment to the language and its traditional culture. Sadly, Nana's husband passed away before I met the family. It is clear that Nana still tries to maintain a Gaelic-centred FLP with her children at some level by still speaking to them in Gaelic; however, as will be shown in the following chapters, Nana's children generally answer her in English and she tends to eventually adopt their preferred code choice of English.

As well as trying to maintain a Gaelic-centred FLP within her own home, Nana worked as a GME teacher once it became available where she taught in Skye. In this role, she recalls how her language practices with pupils often took a similar form to those with her own children: she would speak to them in Gaelic and they would answer her in English. Nana retired shortly before I met the family in 2007 and upon retiring, Nana had more time to

DOI: 10.1057/1057/9781137521811.0008

look after her grandchildren. Nana said that, as was the case in speaking Gaelic to her own children, it was simply 'natural' to speak Gaelic to her grandchildren and she had never intended on doing otherwise. Although Nana's characterisation of her linguistic practices as 'natural' suggests that the decision underlying these practices is unconscious (*cf.* Palviainen and Boyd, 2013, p. 236), I contend that these practices are nonetheless illustrative of the agentative aspect of FLP as discussed in the introduction, and further, that this agency is a result of Nana's beliefs about language and culture and the reflexive relationship between the two. Raising Nana's own children as Gaelic speakers when both she and her husband already used Gaelic in the home and the language was still relatively strong in the community may have seemed more or less 'natural'; however, as discussed in the introduction, because of the ongoing language shift, Nana and her husband's use of Gaelic with their children was *already* somewhat of a marked practice in Skye. Further, both Nana's siblings who also had children did not raise their own children as Gaelic speakers. By the time that Nana's first grandchild came along, using Gaelic with children had become a very marked practice in the community, as highlighted for example by the anecdote related in the Methodology. Nana's description of the practice as 'natural' is therefore an indication of her language ideologies and in essence, her language *loyalty*: for her, it was unthinkable that she would not maintain Gaelic in her family, even though to do this was going against the grains of community norms.

The underlying reasons for Nana's apparent language loyalty towards Gaelic are multifaceted. One reason appears to be Gaelic's association with family; Nana has a strong interest in kinship and genealogy and until Nana's own children became English-dominant, Gaelic had been the primary language in Nana's family for centuries. Gaelic is also the language she spoke with her husband in their many happy years together as well as is the language that she uses in maintaining close relationships with most of her siblings and her cousins. Thus, Gaelic represents part of Nana's connection with her family both past and present. Nana also appears to strongly associate Gaelic with the Isle of Harris, a place to which she is deeply attached. I have visited Harris several times with her and it seems there is a reflexive relationship between Nana's language loyalty and love of Harris: Gaelic is stronger on Harris than it is in Skye and not only does Nana appear to associate Gaelic with Harris and her cousins still living on Harris, but this association reflexively strengthens her deep attachment to the place.

DOI: 10.1057/1057/9781137521811.0008

It is also postulated that Nana's language loyalty also stems from wider beliefs about and participation in a particular culture. Defining a particular 'culture' and the practices that distinguish it from other groups of people is a monumental, if not impossible, undertaking, and often runs the risk of stereotyping; however, the point to be made here is that many of Nana's practices orient to what can be conceptualised as 'traditional' in terms of a particular place and generation. For example, politically, Nana tends to have conservative views; she attends church twice weekly and keeps the Sabbath holy; she listens to the Gaelic radio as her main source of news and entertainment; she always has fresh home-baking on hand in case a visitor should drop in. This is not to imply that Nana has the narrow or static worldview usually (and often mistakenly) ascribed to 'traditional' cultures; Nana is an avid world traveller and often visits friends abroad that she has met on her travels or in hosting at her Bed and Breakfast. She has fully embraced technology as it has advanced; currently, for example, she normally spends at least two hours a day on Facebook, either on her desktop or on her Kindle in the sitting room with the peat fire crackling away. The point in making these observations about Nana is that just as her apparent language loyalty is viewed as her orientation to particular places such as Skye and Harris, as well as to family history/relationships, so too is it viewed as part of her orientation to her generation and a concept of a 'traditional' culture. Thus, speaking Gaelic is not only part of belonging to a particular place, but also to a culture and to a generation situated within that particular place.

However, despite what I am arguing to be Nana's language loyalty in prototypical *Gemeinschaft* terms thus far, I also argue that there is a further, more abstract component to this language loyalty and that this particular component stems in part from Nana's understanding of the fragile state of the Gaelic language. Nana is very eager to speak to and help anyone who is learning Gaelic; not only has she been more than patient with me on my own language learning journey, but on more than one occasion when I have been there, she has had learners of various degrees of proficiency over to her house to speak Gaelic with them. This is not necessarily typical of 'native' practices with L2 speakers, either of Gaelic or other minority languages (see McEwan-Fujita, 2010; Wells, 2011; McLeod, O'Rourke, and Dunmore, 2014; O' Rourke, Pujolar, and Ramallo, 2015), and I contend that this component stems from a more abstract loyalty to *Gaelic as a language* rather than Gaelic as the language of her family and the place in which she lives. I also contend that Nana's

DOI: 10.1057/1057/9781137521811.0008

awareness of the precarious state of Gaelic, which has undoubtedly been compounded by her own experiences in witnessing language shift within her family first-hand, has played a role in formulating the practices by which she orients to a pro-Gaelic ideology. This would explain why, in many ways, Nana's language practices differ from members of other autochthonous communities whose pro-minority language loyalties also render it 'unthinkable' that the next generation cease speaking the minority language, yet unknowingly perpetuate language shift (*cf.* Kulick, 1992; Rindstedt and Aronsson, 2002).

Despite what appears to be Nana's high degree of loyalty, by Nana's own admission and as also suggested by the results of the quantitative view of overall language use, Nana's use of Gaelic in the family has decreased over the years. Nana attributes this perceived decrease in use of Gaelic to being retired from GME for several years and therefore, as she characterises it, being 'out of practice' of responding in Gaelic while being addressed in English. This characterisation suggests that speaking Gaelic to Nana's grandchildren may not be as 'natural' as she may frame it, which is further reflective of the agentative aspect of FLP. This will be elaborated upon in much more detail when looking at the synchronic aspects of language shift within the family. As will also be discussed in greater detail in looking at the synchronic aspect of language shift, Nana is a frequent 'code-drifter'[1] and will frequently adopt her interlocutor's code choice (in nearly all cases, English) within several turns. It is also worth mentioning that Nana's own use of Gaelic is one that employs a great detail of code-switching and morphonological integrations of English lexical items into her Gaelic.

Dolina

Dolina was born in Skye to two Gaelic-speaking parents and like Nana, Gaelic was the language of her home and for the most part, her community while she was growing up. However, unlike Nana, Dolina chose not to raise her own two daughters, one of whom is Peigi, the mother of the third generation, as Gaelic speakers. As will be discussed in greater detail in Peigi's section, this decision played a formative role in Peigi's own decision to learn Gaelic as a second language in adulthood as well as her overtly pro-Gaelic language ideologies. Peigi attributes Dolina's choice not to use Gaelic in the home as stemming from the low prestige of Gaelic and in particular, the exclusion of Gaelic in school when Dolina was growing up. Additionally, the family was living in a larger more urbanised area at the time, where the language shift was more acute. Also, although Peigi's father does speak Gaelic, it is evident from family members' comments that he may not feel particularly comfortable using the language. He did not, for example, take part in my MA study on linguistic proficiency and the reason for this decision appeared to be that he was more of a what Dorian (1981) would refer to as 'semi-speaker' rather than a confident fluent speaker. Throughout her childhood, however, Peigi recalls that Dolina and her husband did occasionally use the language as a secret inter-parent language.

Despite raising her own children as monoglot English speakers, Dolina appears to have undergone an ideological transformation in that she now uses primarily Gaelic both with her two daughters (Peigi's sister also learned Gaelic to fluency) and her grandchildren. As my colleague Timothy Currie Armstrong and I have discussed previously (see Smith-Christmas and Armstrong, 2014), this reality has taken significant effort both on the part of Dolina and her daughters, as they are required to overcome what Spolsky (1991, p. 146) refers to as the 'inertia condition of language choice.' After all, Dolina and her daughters have had to re-negotiate a space (the home) and a relationship (mother-daughter) that were previously mono-lingual English. Both Peigi and her sister are very explicit that they want to create a 'Gaelic-speaking family,' not only with their own children, but among their own nuclear family, in other words, truly 'reversing the language shift' (*cf.* Fishman, 1991) that has already occurred within their family. In turn, Dolina has appeared very willing to partake in her daughters' language maintenance efforts and it is postulated that their explicit pro-Gaelic language ideologies have led to Dolina's apparent ideological transformation and resultant language practices.

Isabel

Isabel is Nana's younger sister by nine years; therefore, although Gaelic was Isabel's home language, only one other child in her age group at school had Gaelic as their home language, which meant that English became her peer group language. This factor is postulated to be one of the main reasons why in the 2009 corpus, Isabel was the lowest user of Gaelic of her generational cohort of eight speakers. Isabel, who has never married or had children, has stayed on the family croft, which she now runs as a Bed and Breakfast. In the years I have known her, Isabel has

DOI: 10.1057/1057/9781137521811.0008

been employed in two different jobs in one of the main urban centres on the island. Neither of these jobs have specifically involved the use of Gaelic, which may also be why, in comparison to Nana, Isabel evidences a relatively low use of Gaelic, as her professional life has been more English language-centred than Nana's. Also in comparison to Nana, Isabel does not appear to maintain as close relationships with her cousins on Harris as Nana does, presumably because the cousins are more Nana's age than Isabel's, which may have made a difference when they were children. This also means that Isabel's daily life appears less Gaelic-centred than Nana's, as Nana's frequent phone calls to her Harris cousins account for a large part of Nana's daily Gaelic use. Further, while Nana is literate in Gaelic through her work in education, Isabel, like many of her generation, is not, and this linguistic disenfranchisement may further play a role in Isabel's low use of the language in comparison to her older sister.

In many ways, Isabel orients to the 'traditional' culture as embedded in a place and generation as Nana does: politically, she tends to be conservative and she attends church twice a week and keeps the Sabbath holy, for example. Like Nana, though, Isabel has also embraced technology and is also an avid world traveller. The two sisters spend most of their free time together; unless she has Bed and Breakfast guests, Isabel will usually have dinner at Nana's house and sometimes spend the night there. She therefore interacts with Nana's children and grandchildren on a frequent basis but unlike Nana, Isabel appears to be more accommodating towards their preferred code choice of English. This practice appears not only to reflect the fact that in many ways English is also Isabel's preferred language, but it is further hypothesised to reflect Isabel's efforts at achieving and maintaining solidarity with Nana's children and grandchildren by using their preferred language. Thus, it is clear to see that Isabel not only is a product of language shift, but that being a product of language shift means that Isabel is more likely to engage in linguistic practices that further perpetuate this shift.

Second generation

Seumas

As mentioned in the section detailing Nana's social and linguistic history, both Nana and her late husband used Gaelic with Seumas during his early years. When Seumas entered school, he reports that he could not

DOI: 10.1057/1057/9781137521811.0008

speak English; the family still recalls with amusement how on his first day of school, one of Seumas' classmates asked Seumas if he had Legos, to which Seumas replied 'Aye *mi* yes.' He learned English very quickly, however, as not only was his classroom instruction in English, but it was strongly his peer group language as well. He recalls being teased by his peers for coming from a Gaelic-speaking family, which was one of the main impetuses in his choice to use English with his siblings Màiri and Aonghas. This practice established English as the inter-sibling language and also eventually led to the practice of answering their parents in English when addressed in Gaelic.

Seumas is now a successful business entrepreneur and as his business has expanded, he is away from Skye more frequently. However, he lives in the same village as Nana and if he is in Skye, he will usually come to Nana's or the third generation's house at least once a day. After leaving school, Seumas had spent a significant amount of time in a large urban area on the mainland for study and then employment. He sometimes speaks of moving back to that particular urban area to further his business. It is clear to me that Seumas orients to a conceptualisation of a modern, successful businessman and it is also clear that he sees English as important in the modern and especially the business world. For example, once I suggested the use of Gaelic in an element of his business but he did not wish to include it because he thought that Gaelic did not afford the necessary prestige required. He also is not in favour of bilingual Gaelic-English signage (either with the Gaelic or the English first) because he thinks it 'confuses tourists.' However, he also has an attachment to Gaelic and wishes to see cultural continuity with his nieces and nephews. In referring to Nana and Peigi's use of Gaelic with the third generation, Seumas once remarked to me that 'I think what they are doing is great' and in a later, separate recorded interview (December 2013) about language and migration, I again asked him if he was pleased that his niece and nephews were being raised as Gaelic speakers. He answered:

> Yes I am, I mean, had you asked me that in 1989 I probably wouldn't have been so bothered about it but I am now because of the way it's gone (.) the language and the area (.) are more kind of- need to protect it now.

The sentiment expressed here coincides with the argument I made in an earlier (2014a) article, in which I posited that Seumas' sporadic use of Gaelic can often be attributed to his latent pro-Gaelic ideology and

DOI: 10.1057/1057/9781137521811.0008

that this ideology is in turn catalysed by the children's negative stances vis-à-vis Gaelic and/or their cultural heritage. It is postulated, therefore, that Seumas' pro-Gaelic ideology stems from a sense that Gaelic is under threat. Seumas also states that if he were ever to have children of his own, he would raise them as Gaelic speakers. Although this is a further orientation to what is referred to as his 'latent' pro-Gaelic ideology, it should be emphasised that his linguistic practices often reflect just how *latent* this ideology is: he generally uses English with his partner (also a Gaelic speaker), his siblings, his peer group, as well as with Nana and her generation. He tends to use Gaelic only in talk directed at the third generation. His marked lower use of Gaelic between the two corpora is not necessarily an indication of his diachronic lower Gaelic use per se, but rather, a reflection of this last premise: because his business commitments meant that he was away for most of the recording sessions, he was not recorded interacting with the third generation, and therefore he does not evidence much use of Gaelic in the 2014 corpus.

Màiri

From Seumas' profile, it is clear to see that Màiri experienced English at an earlier age than him due to, as Nana characterises it, Seumas' 'bringing home the English' from school. While Seumas was raised in a primarily monolingual environment in the home until the age of five, the four year age difference between Màiri and Seumas meant that she experienced English around one year of age due to her brother's use of the language. As detailed earlier, English was the language adopted among the three siblings and they also began to answer their parents in English. Màiri also recalls how she disappointed her father by taking a major European language as a subject instead of Gaelic in school. After leaving school, Màiri worked as an au pair abroad speaking this European language, then went to university in one of the main urban centres in Scotland.

When I met the family in 2007, Màiri was living in the urban centre where she went to university and was working as a highly-skilled professional in her chosen field. It was clear that even though Màiri embraced the urban lifestyle, she maintained strong links with a sense of Gaelic and Hebridean culture as practised and recontextualised within this particular urban environment. For example, she sang in a Gaelic choir and worked in one of the 'Highland' pubs in this area, which is where she met one of her closest friends, also a Gaelic speaker. However,

DOI: 10.1057/1057/9781137521811.0008

Màiri's cultural maintenance did not extend to language, as Màiri and this particular friend use English together. This of course is a marked contrast to Nana's language practices while in an urban environment, as Nana made a point of maintaining Gaelic with her Gaelic-speaking speaking friends. However, for Màiri, English had previously been established as her peer group language in Skye; as well, this lack of active Gaelic use may be an indication of the premise that 'doing' culture can be achieved in other, arguably more superficial ways than using the minority language.

In my 2007 MA thesis, Màiri scored the lowest of her siblings in terms of the Gaelic proficiency tests. This low score was attributed to her extended time in an urban environment and her subsequent self-reported lack of confidence in using the language. In 2008, Màiri moved back to Skye, a decision primarily motivated by a desire to be closer to her family and especially her niece and nephew, who at that time were six and two years old. Shortly after moving back to Skye, Màiri met her partner, who is a Gaelic speaker and Màiri's senior by nearly two decades, and the couple now live about a ten minutes' drive from Nana's house. They use English together, which appears to be mainly a reflex of Màiri's linguistic preference, as her partner is a very confident Gaelic speaker who orients to a very 'traditional' outlook. Màiri has related to me however that although she thinks that she and her partner 'should' use Gaelic, she is reluctant to do so with him because he often corrects her. Màiri has also said that if she were to have her own children, she would take a Gaelic course through Sabhal Mòr Ostaig to gain more confidence in using the language and that her children would receive GME education. Like her brother Seumas, it appears that Màiri's latent pro-Gaelic language ideologies can be awakened; over the two corpora, Màiri and Seumas are mirror images of each other: he used a relatively high degree of Gaelic in the 2009 corpus and an extremely low amount of Gaelic in the 2014 corpus for the reasons discussed in his section. Màiri was the opposite, with very little Gaelic in the 2009 corpus and a relatively high degree in the 2014 corpus. These instances of Gaelic use were mostly an attempt to use Gaelic with Maggie or to use Gaelic with Nana in Maggie's presence on the final night of recording. However, as will be discussed in detail in the next chapter, although Màiri appears to have undergone an ideological transformation over the course of living on Skye again, there are significant barriers to turning these pro-Gaelic language ideologies into actual linguistic practices.

DOI: 10.1057/1057/9781137521811.0008

Aonghas

As can surmised from Seumas and Màiri's sections, Aonghas experienced a moderate to high amount of English in his early years at home, as not only did Seumas and Màiri talk English *to* him, but it was the language the two siblings used together. Like his siblings, English was the language of Aonghas' peer group at school. However, unlike his two older siblings, Aonghas never left for the mainland for an extended period of time. Overall, his interests tend to align more with a 'traditional' culture as situated in a particular place; for example, he now runs the family croft and his business interests tend to be agriculturally oriented. When I first came to the family in 2007, Nana reported that out of her three children, Aonghas was the most willing to speak Gaelic to her. It is hypothesised that this may have been due to the fact that staying in Skye meant that Aonghas had more opportunities to use the language than his siblings did when they lived in mainland urban areas. Further, even though Gaelic could no longer be considered a community language anymore, involvement in crofting is one of the social networks in which Gaelic is most likely to be used and therefore Aonghas' participation in this network would have afforded him additional opportunities to use the language.

It was evident in the initial visits that Aonghas used a high amount of Gaelic with his children. However, by the time I recorded the family in 2009, although Aonghas still used Gaelic with his children, it appeared that these instances of Gaelic use primarily coincide with issuing short directives to the children or in reprimanding them. This particular linguistic practice will be described in greater detail in Chapter 5. Unfortunately, his new employment on the mainland meant that Aonghas was only available for one day of the July 2014 recordings, so it is difficult to compare Aonghas' current use of Gaelic to the 2009 corpus. However, through various observations overall, it appears that Aonghas' use of Gaelic remains consistent with his use in the 2009 corpus in that Gaelic is used mainly in taking an authoritative stance towards his children. For example, just when I had turned off the recording device and was bidding the family farewell for the evening, Aonghas used Gaelic in issuing the following directive to his youngest son Jacob: *Ith do bhiadh* ('Eat your food').

I do not have as close a relationship with Aonghas as I do with his siblings Seumas and Màiri and therefore do not have as much to draw

DOI: 10.1057/1057/9781137521811.0008

on in terms of metalinguistic comments made directly to me over the years. However, in thinking back over my numerous interactions with Aonghas, it appeared that he underwent an ideological transformation just subsequent to the 2009 recordings. This change began when he was involved in a professional course through the medium of Gaelic and then worked in this profession. During this professional course, he appeared very willing to use Gaelic and he even used Gaelic with me. Aonghas' use of Gaelic with me is significant because we had always previously spoken English together, mainly because of my own proficiency issues, but also because English was the language I used with his siblings. Using Gaelic with either Seumas or Màiri would feel false somehow; in the various instances we have used Gaelic together, it is usually treated as a joke or as a means to playfully bring my role as 'family linguist' to the forefront. While Aonghas was involved in this course through the medium of Gaelic, however, it appeared that he was orienting to the concept that is important to use Gaelic, an orientation I attribute to the ideological orientation of the particular institution delivering the professional course. Since taking up employment on the mainland, Aonghas' orientation to this concept seems to have weakened somewhat; however, he is still the only one of the three second generation siblings who will use Gaelic with me in extended conversations.

Peigi

In an earlier work (Smith-Christmas and Armstrong, 2014), my colleague and I refer to Peigi as the 'lynchpin' in brokering intergenerational Gaelic use in the Campbell family. In many ways, Peigi exemplifies Nahirny and Fishman's (1965, p. 312) characterisation of heritage language learning as 'what the son wishes to forget the grandson wishes to remember.' As discussed in Dolina's section, Peigi strongly orients to the ideology that the Gaelic language must be maintained and that it is the duty of Gaelic speakers to use the language with each other and especially with their children. Perhaps ironically, it was Dolina's decision *not* to raise Peigi as a Gaelic speaker that is the main catalyst behind this ideological orientation. Peigi has related to me how witnessing language shift first-hand made her wish to reclaim the language for herself as well as speak it to her children; further, being raised without the language means that she refrains from 'taking it

DOI: 10.1057/1057/9781137521811.0008

[Gaelic] for granted,' as she perceives some native speakers to do. This pro-Gaelic orientation has also been strengthened by the ideological stance of the institution where she learned Gaelic and it is clear that Peigi orients to the '*cleachd i no caill i*' ('use it or lose it') viewpoint that this particular institution takes. Additionally, the fact that Peigi has worked in Gaelic development and education has also presumably played a role in Peigi's overtly pro-Gaelic orientation.

As also discussed in Dolina's section, re-negotiating the language of interaction for conversations between Dolina and her two daughters, and for the daughters between themselves, has entailed a number of challenges. As described in more detail in Smith-Christmas and Armstrong (2014), in terms of linguistic practices, Peigi has cultivated a more or less monolingual style when speaking Gaelic; as well, she consciously attempts to resist code-drifting, as evidenced in the conversational excerpts in the 2014 article and also highlighted for example by Peigi's characterisation of drifting to English as being 'off track,' as she once described her sister as 'good at getting us back on track' when Dolina and Peigi would switch to English. As will be seen in the following chapters, Peigi also tries to adhere to these practices when speaking to her children. She also has tried to actively encourage her children to use Gaelic with each other, as for example, when she told Maggie that 'babies only speak Gaelic' when Maggie's younger brother Jacob was born. Like Nana, Peigi appears diachronically to use less Gaelic and the hypothesised reasons for this will be enumerated upon further in the following chapters. However, unlike Nana, Peigi appears to take a more 'glass half full' rather than 'glass half-empty' approach to her children's Gaelic language use: during the 2009 recording period, it was clear that Nana saw Maggie's Gaelic as language *loss*, in that Maggie did not use as much Gaelic in her early years as David had, while Peigi saw Maggie's development in a more positive light, commenting to me that even if Maggie did not seem to speak much Gaelic, at least she fully understood the language. It is hypothesised that Peigi's outlook is shaped by the fact that Gaelic was hardly used in her own home growing up, and therefore being in an environment where the child can develop at least a passive knowledge of the language is preferable to an environment which precludes this possibility. Further, in looking back on her own language learning trajectory, Peigi postulates that the fact that she at least occasionally heard Gaelic in her home and community was instrumental in her quick path to Gaelic fluency.

DOI: 10.1057/9781137521811.0008

Third generation

David

As mentioned in the Methodology, David used a high degree of Gaelic when I first met the family in 2007 and it was clear that he predominantly used Gaelic when speaking to Nana. The family also likes to tell with great fondness how, when David was under the age of four, his Gaelic was so dominant that it influenced his English. One day he reprimanded a neighbour for frightening Nana's dog, saying, 'You're putting the fright on Archie.' In Gaelic, one would say *tha thu a' cur an eagail air Archie*, which literally translates to 'you're putting the fright on Archie.' However, as mentioned in the Methodology, within approximately the span of a year from 2007 to 2008, David became English-dominant. Upon my first visit in 2008, I asked him (in Gaelic) why he no longer used much Gaelic and he answered something to the effect of *chaidh mi dhan sgoil is chaill mi i* ('I went to school and I lost it [Gaelic]'). As discussed in the introduction, English is the peer group language of GME pupils; therefore, once David's days shifted from primarily being spent with his Gaelic-speaking mother and his two Gaelic-speaking grandmothers to an environment where his teachers spoke Gaelic while his peers spoke English, he 'lost' his Gaelic and shifted to near-monolingual English use. This rapid change and the observation that David's peer group use English are both encapsulated in an e-mail Nana sent to me dated 16 May 2008, which was in answer to some questions I had for her about her experience as a GME teacher:

> it was a permanent struggle to get students to speak Gaelic within their GM groups to say nothing of outwith it—and it is even more obvious to me now as I listen to my young grandson speaking English almost constantly and very automatically now in every situation—and that is since he went to Primary 1 in Gaelic Medium Education! Last week he even said...'I hate Gaelic!'

Not only does this e-mail evidence English as the dominant language among GME students as well as David's own shift toward this norm, but it also evidences the negative attitudes he appears to harbour toward Gaelic, which he also expresses in the 2009 recordings, saying 'No I don't like Gaelic' after Maggie had reported that 'David don't like Gaelic.' When pressed for an answer, however, David only offers 'cause' in response. In

DOI: 10.1057/1057/9781137521811.0008

an earlier interaction where we are playing outside, David also said to me that he did not like Gaelic because it is 'boring.'

Despite his negative attitudes toward Gaelic, David does evidence some use of Gaelic in the 2009 corpus. However, this use appears limited to specific contexts, in particular, to contexts in which David overtly wants something, usually either a physical object or in gaining the attention/praise of his caregivers. For example, two out of David's total five monolingual Gaelic turns in the 2009 corpus involve David trying to attract his mother's attention on the playground ('Mom, *seall mise!*' and 'Mommy, *seall mise*' [Mom/Mommy, look at ME]). Similarly, when his mother praises the good behaviour of David's cousin, David tries to bring attention to his own good behaviour by saying *agus mise* ('and ME, in other words, 'I'm behaving too.'). Two of David's Mixed turns ('Yes, *tha*' [yes] and '*mise* my turn no hot chocolate' [ME]) occur after Nana asks David if he would like a cup of tea or hot chocolate respectively. With the exception of one Mixed turn, the remainder of David's turns that use Gaelic occur when he is trying to mitigate an argument/admonition. For example, when I tell him to 'ask me nicely' to hold a caterpillar that he is trying to put on me, he begins his turn with *am faod tu* ('can you') in beginning his 'nice' question, but then he trails off into English. In another interaction, after Nana has just told David to brush his teeth, David argues with *chan eil mi* ('I'm not'). Similarly, in another interaction, David is apologising to his mother, saying *feumaidh mi feumaidh mi duilich* ('I have to- I have to sorry')[2] and from the overall interaction, it appears that the impetus for this apology is that David needs to make amends for previous misbehaviour so that he can have a biscuit.

One of the reasons why David may think that using Gaelic is likely to help him gain what he wants, whether it is a physical object, attention, or a chance at mitigating an argument is that Gaelic is the language that Nana and Peigi *want* David to speak. All of David's Gaelic or Mixed turns were said either to Nana, Peigi or to me, the researcher, which suggests that David not only understands that Gaelic may be advantageous in gaining what he wants, but specifically, that it is particularly advantageous to use Gaelic with certain caregivers (*cf.* Kopeliovich's [2013, p. 270] example of one of her children writing in Russian, the language that the mother/researcher was trying to maintain, in order to please Kopeliovich). This facet of David's Gaelic use will be discussed in greater detail in Chapter 5 when looking at how Gaelic functions as the 'authoritative' code both within the family and community. As I postulate that

DOI: 10.1057/1057/9781137521811.0008

David's use of Gaelic the 2014 Corpus also relates to this concept, these will also be discussed in greater detail in Chapter 5. Over time, David's overall negative attitudes toward Gaelic as expressed in the 2009 Corpus do not seem to have changed very much. However, he has on different occasions seemed willing to use Gaelic with me and he has not since expressed the overtly negative attitudes he voiced in 2008 and 2009. David is a lively boy and is involved in a variety of activities. He is most interested in football and is a talented athlete. In general, he tends to orient towards the mainstream and youth culture of his particular age group, as became especially apparent to me while conducting the ethnography of his media interests in March 2014. However, he also enjoys more traditionally oriented activities, such as shinty and bagpiping; during the 2014 recordings, for example, he was attending the *Fèis* (week of music classes, dance, and sports activities conducted through the medium of Gaelic) and seemed to highly enjoy it.

Maggie

When she was younger, particularly in the 2009 recordings, Maggie was a very lively and vocal child. However, Maggie never achieved the same level of fluency of Gaelic that her brother David (4;7 at the time) had achieved when I first met the family in 2007. In the 2009 corpus (when Maggie was 3;4), Maggie's productive capabilities in Gaelic consist primarily of single lexical items; she uses 24 different Gaelic nouns, three Gaelic question words, 13 Gaelic adjectives, three Gaelic verbs, one Gaelic conjunction, two Gaelic prepositions and one Gaelic determiner. In total, these 44 different Gaelic lexical items were used over a total of 90 turns. In 20 cases, these lexical items were used by an adult in a prior utterance. In the remaining 70 cases, however, Maggie produces the word spontaneously. Generally, these lexical items either occur as the single element of the turn (particularly in the case of the question words, such as *carson* ['why']) or as a single element as an otherwise-English turn (for example, 'I need to get my *clachan*' ['stones']; 'I want *bainne*' ['milk']; 'Because my *tòn* is *fuar*' ['bum/cold']). Maggie also evidences productive use of Gaelic syntactic structures, particularly of the *aig* ('at') structure, where *aig* plus a noun indicates possession (for example, *taigh aig Nana* [Nana's house]) and she also can use the first person prepositional pronoun form of *aig* in the emphatic form (*aig* + *mo*[my] = *agam*;

DOI: 10.1057/1057/9781137521811.0008

+ *sa* [emphatic form] = *agamsa*), as in one instance, Maggie says 'mommy *agamsa*,' indicating that she is referring to *her* mommy, not anyone else's mommy. Maggie also has the ability to use simple, syntactically complete units – in other words, complete sentences – such as *cà' bheil e?* ('where is it?') and *bha Sean* okay ('Grandfather was okay').[3]

Many of Maggie's lexical mixes occur in situations in which she is playing and refer to objects that become important in the play sequence, such as what she is playing with (for example, *clachan* 'stones' or *spaid* 'spade') or items she is counting (for example, the 'legs' [in other words, the stems] on some flowers, in which she produces 'one *cas* two *cas*' ['leg']) or referring to illustrations/events in a story (for example, *fliuch* 'wet' and *gealach* 'moon'). The other instances of Maggie's Gaelic use, however, appear to coincide with Maggie's argumentative stance vis-à-vis her caregivers, which bears some similarity to her brother David's use of the language. Maggie's use of Gaelic in this particular context often takes the form of Maggie's insertion of a lexical item her caregiver has used in a previous utterance into Maggie's own utterance (for example, 'I'm not putting it in my *beul*' ['mouth'] after Nana has just admonished Maggie for putting a candle in her mouth or 'wee bit *brèagha*' [pretty] after Nana has asserted that the Play-Doh rose I have made for Maggie is pretty and Maggie disagrees). Other examples of Maggie's use of Gaelic in argumentative contexts occur in an interaction in which she has spilled bubbles over an important-looking letter addressed to her father. She spontaneously produces 'Daddy will be *fiadhaich*?' ['angry'] and then later on in the interaction declares that the letter is dry with 'This is *tioram*' ['dry']. Further, her use of *carson* ('why'), which was her most frequently used question word in the 2009 corpus (11 occurrences), was often used in an argumentative manner, for example, in questioning a caregiver's directive to her. Maggie's use of Gaelic in an argumentative context is hypothesised to stem from several realities: first, as will be discussed in greater detail in Chapter 5, Gaelic is often constructed as the authority code both within the family and community; secondly, as discussed in David's section, the fact that Maggie's caregivers *want* her to speak Gaelic may prompt her to see Gaelic as a valuable resource in mitigating disciplinary action. Related to this second hypothesis is also the fact that her caregivers often find her lexical insertions amusing, which may also be useful in deflecting trouble. For example, in the interaction where Maggie spills bubbles on her father's letter the fact that her earlier declaration of 'I'm going to *dùin* the *dòras*' ('close'/'door') clearly amused

DOI: 10.1057/1057/9781137521811.0008

Nana and Seumas may have been instrumental in Maggie's later use of code-mixing in her attempts to mitigate the trouble caused by the spilt bubbles.

By the 2014 corpus, Maggie's productive use of Gaelic had decreased by nearly a half from 11.03% (75 turns) in the 2009 corpus to 5.43% of her turns (15 turns). Further, seven of these turns were only semi-spontaneous in that code choice was on some level dictated; in one interaction Maggie's great-aunt Isabel directs Maggie to use Gaelic by saying 'tell me something in Gaelic then' and Maggie subsequently embarks on telling about her day at the *Fèis*. Although these instances of Gaelic are only semi-spontaneous, they reveal that while Maggie does not *use* the language much as an eight year old, she nonetheless has gained linguistic competence in the language over the years, as seen from the excerpt below:

---

1 Maggie *an ua:ir sin (1.2) an uair sin (0.8)*
             then   then

         chaidh sinn (1.8) air ais gu boc/sa (1.3)
            we went   back to box [class, i.e. accordion class]

         agus: (1.2) an uair sin (2.8) chaidh sinn gu iomain (1.4)
            and   then   we went to shinty

         's choisich sinn air ais (0.7) (warming?) *(1.9) no (0.4)*
            and we walked back   or(or English 'no')

         chaidh sinn ann am (0.9) a' mhini- (0.4) bini- *(2.5) mhin- (2.2)* eh *(5.3)* bus
            we went in the   the mini-   min

This excerpt shows Maggie's ability to use syntactically complex structures in Gaelic, namely, correct VSO order in forming complete sentences. She can use the past tense (evidenced by leniting *coisich* [initial [k]] to *choisich* [initial [x]] and it is worth noting that the verb 'to go' in Gaelic is irregular (meaning that the past of *rach* is *chaidh*). Her repairs in the word 'mini-bus' are interesting from an acquisitional and contact point of view. She appears to have acquired the rule that definite nouns following a prepositional phrase require lenition,[4] as she begins with what looks like an indefinite prepositional construction (*ann am* 'in'), then appears to attempt and frame it as definite (*a' mhini*). As both [b] and [m] lenite to [v] (albeit a nasalised [v] in the case of [m] lenition), it is possible that Maggie is searching for the 'original' sound in the word mini-bus (*cf.* Dorian, 2015 for a similar discussion).[5] I suggest that this indicates that Maggie has indeed acquired a high degree of linguistic competence in terms of Gaelic's morphosyntactic structure. However,

DOI: 10.1057/1057/9781137521811.0008

the frequent pauses and repairs in this passage indicate that although Maggie may have a high level of Gaelic in terms of the structural components of the language, her overall fluency is lower, a hypothesis which is further supported by the fact that Maggie initially did not want to relate her day at the *Fèis* in Gaelic because she characterised it as 'hard.'

Over the years, Maggie has indexed rather ambiguous attitudes toward Gaelic. As will be seen in a conversational excerpt in the next chapter, at one point in the 2009 corpus, Maggie states: 'I like *Beurla*. I don't like Gaelic' ('English'). However, in another point in the 2009 corpus, Maggie declares that she likes Gaelic but that her brother does not (David then counters that with claiming that 'yesterday' Maggie said that she did not like Gaelic). Although Maggie's declaration of liking Gaelic may be simply a way to create animosity between her and her brother, the ambiguity of these two declarations coincides with my observations of her language attitudes over the years. Sometimes she has appeared to have positive attitudes toward the language as suggested, for example, by specific acts, such as bringing me a book to read to her in Gaelic. It is posited that these apparent positive attitudes toward Gaelic are owed at least in part to Maggie's experience in GME, as she has attained literacy through the medium of Gaelic and she enjoys reading and writing in Gaelic. In contrast to David, school appears to have had a positive impact on Maggie's Gaelic abilities, as it has helped her attain linguistic competence in the language as well as helped her foster positive attitudes toward the language. Maggie excels in school and her teacher emphasised in Maggie's most recent report card (2015) that Maggie is a fluent Gaelic speaker. However, despite this fluency, Maggie does not evidence much use of the language of her own accord, which suggests that she may harbour other, less positive attitudes toward the language.

When she was younger, Maggie was extremely lively. Now, however, she is quieter; as Nana puts it, Maggie is very 'ladylike.' Maggie's interests appear to lie in artistic activities, such as crafts, drawing pictures, and writing stories. She also has an interest in traditional cultural activities, particularly in traditional music.

Jacob

Jacob is the only child in this study I have known since birth and also the most English-dominant of the three children during their early years. Jacob was 4;0 in the 2014 corpus and his Gaelic lexical use was restricted to a total of nine Gaelic lexical items (seven nouns, one adjective, and one verb) over the total of 21 Gaelic and Mixed turns. The lexical items that comprise Jacob's Gaelic use either occur as the sole element of a turn, for example, when he says *bàta* [boat] upon seeing boats in the harbour, or as a single lexical item in a non-sentential structure, for example '*ola-* oil in there,' in which he repeats Nana's use of *ola* ('oil'), then repeats it in English. Several of Jacob's turns coded as Mixed are actually metalinguistic arguments in which he tells the adult not to use a particular Gaelic word, for example 'no not *iasg*' ('fish;' in which he tells Nana not to use the Gaelic equivalent for 'fish' or 'no not *taigh-bheag*,' in which Jacob tells me not to use the Gaelic for 'toilet' in telling him that Nana is in the toilet.). Unlike Maggie, who was able to integrate Gaelic lexical items into syntactically complex English structures such as canonical full sentences, Jacob's language use does not evidence this integration ability. The only utterances that show any integration of Gaelic lexical items into more complex English syntactic structures are 'look *bàta eile!*' and 'where's *bàta eile?*' Although in the second example it is easy to understand what Jacob means, the lack of a determiner makes it seem less 'correct,' so to speak, as in Gaelic, one would expect *am* to precede '*bàta*' (making the sentence 'where's the other boat?'). In Maggie's mixing, for example, she accounted for determiners by saying things like 'I'm going to *dùin* the *dòras*' ('close' 'door'), in which she simply slotted in the English determiner for its Gaelic equivalent. It is possible in the case of Jacob's *bàta eile* that this particular phrase has been re-lexified into one unit. It therefore would not indicate any syntactic productive capabilities beyond single lexical item use. Such is also argued to be the case when he uses the correct determiner + noun combination in producing 'Gina's away in *Na Hearadh*' (Harris).

Jacob's productive use of Gaelic is very low and the Gaelic he does produce does not indicate a high level of linguistic competence in the language. He also evidences overtly negative attitudes toward the language; for example, the Mixed turns in which he tells Nana or me not to use a particular Gaelic lexical item appear to be motivated by the desire not to hear Gaelic spoken. Further, in the December 2014 recordings, Jacob tells his great-aunt Isabel three times not to read the Noah's Ark story in Gaelic (it is written in English but Isabel is reading it in Gaelic). Isabel capitulates and reads the story in English, but when she asks Jacob *dè a' Ghàidhlig a th' air* hay? ('what's the Gaelic for 'hay'?), he

DOI: 10.1057/1057/9781137521811.0008

very adamantly says, 'Don't say it in Gaelic.' Overall, his attitudes toward the language appear much more overtly negative than either of his siblings' were around that age or at the age they are now.

Summary

This chapter has discussed the Campbell family's FLP from a diachronic perspective and has shown how the creation of the Gaelic-centred FLP involving David, Maggie, and Jacob has been brought about by different FLPs created long before these three speakers were born. Perhaps, ironically, the main impetus of the Gaelic-centred FLP with the third generation is due mostly to Dolina's English-dominated FLP with Peigi. The other main guiding force in the pro-Gaelic FLP is Nana, whose Gaelic-centred FLP with her own children was successful in that the second generation Campbell siblings grew up speaking Gaelic, even though they do not use currently use the language very often. In many ways, the third generation Campbell siblings appear to mirror the second generation (and to some extent, the first generation siblings in terms of Nana and Isabel) in that Gaelic use decreases with each child. However, this decrease in Gaelic with siblings is not static and the chapter has detailed how individual speakers have changed their use and orientations toward the language over time. The chapter also has detailed how on the whole, it appears that there is currently less Gaelic used in the family than five years ago. The following chapter examines the synchronic micro-level processes hypothesised to have brought this reality into being.

Notes

1   Although this practice may also be referred to simply as 'code-switching,' 'code-drifting' is analogous to what Gafaranga (2010, 2011) refers to as 'talking language shift into being' (for example, in Nana's case, taking up her interlocutor's preferred code choice of English for multiple turns). This is will be discussed in greater detail in Chapter 4.

2   The awkward syntax in the English translation suggests that this is a non-standard use of Gaelic.

DOI: 10.1057/1057/9781137521811.0008

3   Even though the word 'okay' is an English word, it is so ubiquitous in Gaelic that if this sentence would have been uttered by a first generation member, I would have coded it as monolingual Gaelic.

4   The correct construction would either be *ann am mini-bus* (in a mini-bus) or *anns a' mhini-bus* (in the mini-bus), depending on whether Maggie was framing the mini-bus as definite or indefinite.

5   I am grateful to my colleagues at the University of Edinburgh discussing this point after one of the Soillse seminars in 2015, particularly for the example of using the French word *valise* ('suitcase') in Breton, in helping me arrive at this particular interpretation.

DOI: 10.1057/1057/9781137521811.0008

4

Building and Dismantling an FLP at the Micro-Level

Abstract: *This chapter discusses how the Gaelic-centred FLP is created and then subsequently dismantled at the micro-level of conversation. The chapter argues that Nana and Peigi set up the Gaelic-centred FLP by maintaining 'dual-lingualism' (cf. Saville-Troike, 1987) and also by using Gaelic in explicitly child-centred interactions. The chapter then discusses how although dual-lingualism is a maintenance strategy, it is also the tip of the dismantlement process according to Lanza's (1997) continuum. The chapter then uses Gafaranga's (2010) concept of 'talking language shift into being' to discuss how caregivers inadvertently further dismantle the Gaelic-centred FLP. The chapter concludes by discussing the barriers the second generation members would face in trying to minimise their role in perpetuating language shift.*

Keywords: caregiver discourse strategies; dual-lingualism; talking language shift into being

Smith-Christmas, Cassie. *Family Language Policy: Maintaining an Endangered Language in the Home.* Basingstoke: Palgrave Macmillan, 2016. DOI: 10.1057/9781137521811.0009.

A 'stand your ground' approach to language choice

The last chapter discussed how Nana and Peigi's social and linguistic experiences have shaped their language ideologies and how these ideologies in turn play an important role in these two main actors' creation and maintenance of the Gaelic-centred FLP. Perhaps not surprisingly, the primary way that Nana and Peigi maintain the Gaelic-centred FLP is by speaking Gaelic to the children. In doing so, what normally emerges is what Saville-Troike (1987) terms 'dual-lingual' interactions, in which one interlocutor uses one code and the other interlocutor uses another code. This, Saville-Troike argues, is qualitatively different from truly bilingual conversations, where interlocutors are apt to code-switch throughout the interaction, or what she refers to as 'dilingual' conversations, which take the same format as dual-lingual conversations, but where neither interlocutor understands the other's code. Dual-lingual conversations are also common in Gafaranga's (2010) study of Rwandans in Belgium, to which he ascribes the term 'parallel mode', the existence of which he (2010, p. 266) characterises as a 'maintenance-oriented strategy'. An example of one such dual-lingual/parallel mode conversation is seen in the following excerpt, which is drawn from the 2009 corpus and takes place as Nana, Maggie (who is 3;4 at the time) and I are driving to Nana's rental cottage in Harris:

EXAMPLE 4.1   *Lolly*

1	Maggie	well I saw it (2.0) will we be at your house Nana?=
2	Nana	=eh?
3	Maggie	we nearly at your house
4	Nana	*cha mhòr nach bi sinn fada (.5) cha bhi sinn fada (2.4)*
		`we won't be long        we won't be long`
		tha sinn a' dol sìos ann a sheo
		`we're going down here`
5	Maggie	what?
6	Nana	*tha sinn a' dol sìos a seo far a bheil an làraidh*
		`we're going down here where the lorry is`
7	Maggie	lolly?
8	Nana	*[[seall an làraidh a tha seo]*
		`see the lorry that's here`
9	Maggie	[[what's a lolly]
10	Nana	*làraidh ann a sheo*
		`a lorry here`
11	Maggie	what lolly? mmm? mmm? mmm? what you doing? why you going down here?
12	Nana	*seo far a bheil an taigh againn*
		`this is where our house is`

DOI: 10.1057/9781137521811.0009

Here, Nana maintains the use of Gaelic (Turns 4, 6, 8, 10) even though Maggie continually speaks in English (Turns 1, 3, 5, 9, and 11). Further, the use of Gaelic is also maintained despite the fact that Maggie's Turns 5, 7, and 9 could be interpreted as 'medium requests' (Gafaranga, 2010), whereby the adult takes the child's request for clarification to be an implicit demand to switch to the majority language, the underlying motivation for which is the child's low proficiency in the minority language (see also Pan [1995, p. 326] for a similar observation about Mandarin-speaking parents in the US). The adjacency pair between Turns 4 and 5, where Maggie asks 'what' in Turn 5, bears striking similarity to Gafaranga's (2010, p. 242) example where, following the adult's use of Kinyarwanda, the child speaks French, asking *quoi* ('what'). In Gafaranga's example, the adult perceives that the child has not understood what has been said in the minority language Kinyarwanda and therefore switches to the majority language French. Maggie's 'what' in Turn 5 could be interpreted similarly; however, unlike the adult in Gafaranga's example, Nana does not switch to the majority language. It appears that Nana is unwilling to switch languages in spite of Maggie's apparent proficiency issues; in Turns 7 and 9, it becomes evident that Maggie does not understand the Gaelic word for 'lorry,' a borrowing based on English. Despite this communicative barrier, however, Nana does not capitulate to Maggie's implicit medium request. Instead of translating the word *làraidh* into English, Nana speaks Gaelic in trying to elucidate the meaning of *làraidh* by using visual cues, such as directing Maggie's attention to the lorry at the turnoff.

From the analysis of this excerpt, it is clear that although, as discussed in Chapter 3, Nana may characterise her use of Gaelic with her grandchildren as 'natural,' in terms of the mechanics of the interaction, speaking Gaelic to them takes a more 'stand your ground' approach on Nana's part than her characterisation may suggest. This is further illustrated in the following excerpt, which is drawn from a the 2014 corpus and again, involves Nana, her grandchild (Jacob in this particular excerpt, who is 4;0 at the time) and I riding in the car, this time on our way to lunch at one of our favourite restaurants in Skye:

EXAMPLE 4.2   *Mainly Music*

1	Jacob	what- where is this? (.) what's that?
2	Nana	*a bheil thu ag aithneachadh an àite ud?*
		do you recognise that place over there?
3	Jacob	what's that?

DOI: 10.1057/9781137521811.0009

4	Nana	*dè bhiodh shios an siud? dè bha shios an siud?*
		what used to be there? what was there?
5	Jacob	what's that?
6	Nana	eh? *dè bh' ann=*
		what was there
7	Jacob	=I don't know
8	Nana	*bhiodh tu dol ann* (.) M-
		you used to go there
9	Jacob	Mai(n)ly Music
10	Nana	Mainly Music (.) *sheadh* (.) Mainly music
		uh-huh
11	Jacob	that's not called Mainly Music

It is clear to see that this particular example is nearly identical in form to the interaction between Nana and Maggie five years ago: Nana speaks in Gaelic and Jacob answers in English. Also like the excerpt involving Maggie, Jacob's repetition of 'what's that' in Turns 3 and 5 could be interpreted as a medium request, as repeating the coda to his first turn suggests that he has not understood what Nana has said. As in the excerpt with Maggie, again Nana stands her ground in terms of language choice. She does, however, use English in repeating (and encouraging, although she only says 'M' in Turn 8) Jacob to say the name of 'Mainly Music,' an activity that he used to attend. Nana's repetition of Jacob's utterance is analysed as a means to confirm that his utterance is correct in content, as well as implicitly praise him for this correct utterance.

The agentative aspects of dual-lingualism

In looking at Nana's language use with her grandchildren compared to her use with adults throughout the two corpora, several key observations emerge that further support the hypothesis that using the dual-lingual/parallel mode approach takes both agency and effort on Nana's part and may not be as 'natural' as she characterises it. First, related to the premise that these two excerpts involve implicit medium requests due to comprehension issues on the child's part, it should be emphasised that in Nana's conversations with adult interlocutors, code-switching between languages is often Nana's first recourse when she encounters any communicative trouble. For example, in a lengthy narrative about

DOI: 10.1057/9781137521811.0009

a potential trip to the Flannan Isles Nana frequently draws on code-switching in attempting to make this complicated story comprehensible to her interlocutor (Smith-Christmas, 2012, 2014b). It is therefore not unreasonable to hypothesise that when speaking to her grandchildren, it may be tempting for Nana to draw on code-switching in making herself understood, especially when the children have indexed her code choice as problematic. However, as seen from these excerpts, Nana resists the urge to code-switch when communicative trouble arises, which is postulated to be a facet of her 'stand your ground' approach to language choice as a means to maintaining the Gaelic-centred FLP. Further, in general, Nana's Gaelic utterances said to her grandchildren tend to be more monolingual than her utterances directed at adults. Although in conversing with her grandchildren the content of what Nana is saying tends to be simpler and therefore she does not have as great a need to draw on the complicated indexical manoeuvres that tend to prompt her use of code-switching, it is argued that the monolingual nature of Nana's child-directed utterances is also a reflex of the 'stand your ground' approach to language choice rather than a consequence of the fact that child-directed conversations are linguistically and pragmatically simpler than adult conversations.

Finally, using the dual-lingual/parallel mode goes against Nana's apparent preference for same-language interactions, which Auer (1984) hypotheses is a trait shared among bilingual speakers and accounts for the fact that code choice negotiations normally result in both interlocutors taking up the same code. As it has been emphasised that Nana is a frequent code-switcher, in Nana's case this same-language preference is best understood using Gafaranga's (2000) modification of the concept to equate to same *medium*, rather than same *language* preference. Gafaranga argues that in the Rwandan-Belgian context, the juxtaposition of codes is drawn not across linguistic lines, but rather, that the two modes of operation are a mixed Kinyarwanda-French medium and a monolingual French medium (which is the medium the child in the first example mentioned in this chapter was trying to negotiate). For Nana, it is argued that the two mediums are a mixed Gaelic-English medium and a monolingual English medium. As the majority of her interlocutors prefer English, this means that the code negotiation is unidirectional and Nana adopts the medium of monolingual English as opposed to a mixed Gaelic-English medium. This is exemplified in the following, which occurs in the same interaction from which the example 'Lolly' is

DOI: 10.1057/9781137521811.0009

drawn. Here, Nana pulls off the road at a layby to take a phone call from her sister Isabel and Isabel relates the news from Skye:

EXAMPLE 4.3   *Photography course*

1	Nana	*chan eil /\oh well am fac' thu duine an-diugh?*
		no did you see anyone today?
2	Isabel	oh *chan fhaca* Tina's coming home today
		didn't see
3	Nana	is she what's wrong?
4	Isabel	/\e::h .hh she was supposed to be doing
		a photography course *thuirt iad*
		they said
5	Nana	uh-huh
6	Isabel	for a /week
7	Nana	I see:
8	Isabel	and that was cancelled [[there] weren't enough in for it=
9	Maggie	[[(Nana)]
10	Nana	=in Glasgow
11	Isabel	uh-huh
12	Nana	oh I see

It is clear to see how Nana follows Isabel's turn-internal switch to English in Turn 2 with an English-language utterance in Turn 3. With the exception of the coda to Isabel's Turn 4 (*thuirt iad* 'they said'), Isabel continues in English and Nana aligns with Isabel's code choice in her subsequent utterances. This pattern is very common throughout the corpus and it is therefore argued that Nana's adoption of dual lingualism/ parallel mode with her grandchildren goes against her overall preference for same medium interaction as exemplified in this conversation between Nana and Isabel. This, coupled with the observation that Nana's child-directed utterances tend to be more monolingual overall than those said to adults, suggests that upholding the dual-lingual/parallel mode therefore not only entails a suppression of Nana's preference for same-medium interactions but also suppression of her habitual code-switching. In its place emerges a monolingual Gaelic medium. Although it is not surprising that Nana's linguistic practices with children may differ from her linguistic practices with adults, these observations further illustrate that creating and maintaining the Gaelic-centred FLP is an agentative and conscious process on Nana's part. Like the Kinyarwanda adults in Gafaranga's (2010)

DOI: 10.1057/9781137521811.0009

article, it appears that Nana is highly aware that in conversing with her grandchildren, same-medium use can only go one way and that is in favour of the majority language, as her grandchildren will not respond in the minority language, which is due primarily to their lack of linguistic competence in Gaelic, particularly in the case of Jacob. In conversing with English-dominant adults, Nana is also arguably aware that same-medium adoption is weighted towards English; however, it is conjectured that when talking to adults rather than her grandchildren, Nana does not perceive the stakes to be as high. After all, the adults' acquisition process has been completed and Nana no longer has the power to influence it; further, the adults' language preferences are already well-entrenched. In her grandchildren's case, however, persistent use of Gaelic has the potential to benefit the third generation's acquisition and use of the language.

It is argued that the concepts of agency and consciousness are also at work when looking at how Peigi orients to the Gaelic-centred FLP by using the dual-lingual/parallel mode. This is illustrated in the following excerpt drawn from the 2009 corpus in which Nana and Peigi are asking Maggie where has placed her toy motorbike (which Maggie refers to as her 'mo-bo bike.'). They also use Gaelic to discuss a mutual acquaintance's wedding among themselves.

EXAMPLE 4.4   *Mo-bo bike*

1	Maggie	nobody look at my mo-bo bike
2	Nana	oh *tha e a-muigh=*
		it's outside
3	Maggie	=no
4	Peigi	*an tug thu a-staigh e?*
		did you bring it inside?
5	Maggie	°yeah
6	Nana	so *cà' bheil a' bhanais [[aig Fergus?]*
		where is Fergus' wedding?
7	Maggie	[[in the back door Mommy]
8	Peigi	[[*shìos ann an Slèite]*
		down in Sleat
9	Nana	[[*Slèite]*
10	Maggie	mommy it's that in-it in in the back door
11	Peigi	well *cùm an sin e*
		keep it there
12	Nana	mmm-hmm
13	Maggie	why?

DOI: 10.1057/9781137521811.0009

As in the previous examples, this excerpt illustrates the dual-lingual/ parallel mode paradigm, where both Nana and Peigi use Gaelic in their utterances directed at Maggie while she responds to them in English. Although Maggie's English responses are not as overtly marked in terms of medium request as in the last two examples, her use of English still could be interpreted as an implicit request to switch to a monolingual English medium. However, neither interlocutor yields to this implicit request. As discussed in the last section, this takes a certain amount of effort on Nana's part and it is argued that it takes even more effort on Peigi's part, given that Gaelic is not her native language nor the language in which she was socialised as a child. Although Peigi is a fully proficient bilingual, various metalinguistic comments made to me over the years indicate that not surprisingly, because she learned Gaelic in adulthood, Peigi feels that English is her more dominant language. When I first met the family in 2007, she related to me that as David had started speaking more English, it was becoming harder to speak Gaelic to him. However, as seen here and in other examples to follow, Peigi still tries to maintain the dual-lingual/parallel mode with her children.

In addition to the possible linguistic and especially interactional difficulties that arise in maintaining the dual-lingual/parallel mode, there are the emotional challenges as well. Nana finds it 'demoralising' that her grandchildren do not speak Gaelic, which is hypothesised to have played a role in her apparent decrease of Gaelic over the years. In the December 2014 interview, Isabel describes speaking Gaelic to David while he answers her in English as a 'barrier (.) or a friction (1.2) [...] it kinda gets your hackles up if you know what I mean.' This description may explain why, in addition to English generally being her preferred language, Isabel does not often use the dual-lingual paradigm when interacting with Nana's grandchildren. This feeling of friction caused by maintaining dual-lingualism has also been mentioned by Seumas and Màiri as well.

In this excerpt, Nana and Peigi also use Gaelic together in discussing the topic of the wedding. This use of Gaelic is emblematic of Peigi's stated belief that she wishes to create a *Gaelic-speaking family* and that doing so means not just speaking directly to her children in Gaelic but also to any family member willing to use the language with her. As discussed in Chapter 3, as a heritage speaker of Gaelic, Peigi has had to overcome a number of challenges, such as re-negotiating relationships previously built through the medium of English. This particular excerpt shows how, in addition to maintaining dual-lingualism/parallel mode, Peigi

DOI: 10.1057/9781137521811.0009

and Nana also maintain the Gaelic-centred FLP by providing Gaelic input and a context for Gaelic use beyond caregiver–child dyads. As will be discussed later in the chapter, the cumulative effect of other family members *not* engaging in this practice is one of the contributing factors to the dismantlement of the Gaelic-centred FLP.

This section has described the challenges Nana and Peigi face when maintaining the dual-lingual/parallel mode. It has also described how employing this linguistic practice as a means to maintaining the Gaelic-centred FLP requires both agency and effort on the part of the caregivers. The following section looks at how Nana and Peigi further attempt to maintain the Gaelic-centred FLP by explicitly using Gaelic in child-centred contexts.

Encouraging the use of Gaelic in child-centred contexts

It evident from the corpora and my observations that in addition to trying to maintain the dual-lingual/parallel mode paradigm, Peigi and Nana also try to encourage Gaelic in specifically child-centred contexts. Encouraging the use of Gaelic in specifically child-centred contexts also seems to be the main way that Seumas and Màiri, whose orientation to the Gaelic-centred FLP is far weaker than Nana's or Peigi's, occasionally participate in its maintenance. Both Maggie and Jacob appear to highly enjoy counting at the ages of around three to four. In the 2009 corpus there are three instances in which Maggie is encouraged to count in Gaelic and she does so enthusiastically, which is not very characteristic of her Gaelic use as a whole. One of these instances of counting in Gaelic is initially prompted by Seumas' use of Gaelic in stating that Maggie excels at counting. Nana then capitalises on Seumas' (rare) use of Gaelic and begins counting in Gaelic. Maggie subsequently follows Nana's lead, as seen below:

EXAMPLE 4.5   *Counting*

1	Nana	*a bheil thu fhèin a' dol a thòiseachadh air leughadh?*
		are you yourself going to start reading?
2	Seumas	*tha i <u>math</u> air <u>cunntas</u>*
		she's good at counting
3	Nana	*/\tha (.) aon*
		yes (.) one
4	Maggie	*dhà*
		two

DOI: 10.1057/9781137521811.0009

It is argued that in using Gaelic, Seumas is making an implicit request for Maggie to use Gaelic in counting. After all, Seumas does not evidence a high use of Gaelic and so therefore his use of Gaelic is 'marked' (*cf.* Myers-Scotton, 1988). Nana appears to correctly interpret the request implicit in Seumas' marked use of language and prompts Maggie to count in Gaelic. Unlike the other instances of Nana's first-pair part eliciting an English second-pair part from Maggie as seen in the previous examples, here Maggie responds to Nana's use of Gaelic with Gaelic. It is argued that this exception to the habitual dual-lingual paradigm is not coincidental, but rather, occurs because both Seumas and Nana are highly aware that counting is one of the contexts in which Maggie is *most likely* to use Gaelic, and therefore, the caregivers actively create opportunity for Maggie to productively use her minority language. Similarly, in the December 2014 recordings (when Jacob was 4;4), Jacob begins to count items in a storybook and Màiri, who is reading him the story in English, asks him 'can you do it in Gaelic?' Jacob then switches to Gaelic and manages to count until 29 in Gaelic. Although the content of Màiri's request is in Gaelic, it nonetheless encourages the child's productive use of Gaelic and it is argued that like the previous example from the 2009 corpus, Màiri is highly aware that counting is one of contexts most likely to result in the child's productive use of the minority language.

Use of Gaelic in storytime interactions

Both of the counting examples occur in interactions which also involve storytime, which is another way that Nana and Peigi, and occasionally Seumas and Màiri, orient to the Gaelic-centred FLP. This orientation takes the form of reading children's books in Gaelic that are written in English. This is a practice I have witnessed since I first came to the family in 2007 and which is documented in the 2009 corpus and the December 2014 recordings. As discussed in my 2014a article, however, the opportunity to read the story in Gaelic does not come without a struggle; similar to the dual-lingual/parallel mode conversations discussed in the last section, here too Nana must take a 'stand your ground' approach to language choice. In this excerpt, which is also shown (in a slightly truncated form) in the 2014a article, Nana implicitly offers Maggie a choice of language for the story. Maggie decides on Nana's non-preferred choice of English, which then leads to an argument about which language the story should be read in. As seen below, Nana eventually reads the story in Gaelic:

DOI: 10.1057/9781137521811.0009

EXAMPLE 4.6   *I like Beurla (from Smith-Christmas, 2014a)*

1	Maggie	=nobody (.) there read <u>that</u> book
2	Nana	*dè fear?*
		which one?
3	Maggie	<u>that</u> one.
4	Nana	*ann a(n) <u>Gàidhlig</u>*
		in Gaelic
5	Maggie	yes
6	Nana	oh */glè mhath*
		very good
7	Maggie	no *B- Beurla*
		English
8	Nana	eh?
9	Maggie	*Beurla*
		English
10	Nana	*Beurla?*
		English?
11	Maggie	yes
12	Nana	*carson?*
		why?
13	Maggie	I */like Beurla* (.) I don't like (.) *Gàidhlig* (.)
		English
		can you read it?
14	Seumas	((repressed laughter (0.7)))
15	Maggie	(?)
16	Seumas	you don't like <u>*Gàidhlig*</u>?
17	Maggie	WH< aye > WH
21	Nana	*carson?*
		why?
22	Maggie	'cause I like *Beurla* (.) so what?
		English
23	(10.3)	(Seumas and Nana trying not to laugh)
	Maggie	so what? so what? so what?
24	Seumas	you don't like *Gàidhlig*?
25	Maggie	d- no- o
26	Seumas	no?
28	Maggie	so what? so what Nana?
29	Nana	*bheir mise <u>so</u> <u>what</u> ort*
		I'll give you a 'so what'
30	Maggie	I want to read *Beurla*
31	Seumas	*a:h leugh ann a(n) Gàidhlig e Nana*
		read it in Gaelic
32	Maggie	no=
33	Nana	*=leughaidh Nana ann a(n) Gàidhlig iad*
		Nana will read them in Gaelic
34	Maggie	no (.) I to want ((to leave it))
35	Nana	*o:::h* (.) *dhùi:\sg Teddy Beag 's thòisich e air sreothart/aich.*
		Little Teddy woke up and he started to sneeze

DOI: 10.1057/9781137521811.0009

In this example, the question of what language to have the story in is only implicit, as Nana's confirmation check that the story will be *ann a(n) Gàidhlig* in Turn 4 is not a direct question of what language to read the story in. However, Maggie uses this opportunity to assert her code choice by (somewhat ironically) stating that she wants the story in *Beurla* ('English'). Nana however questions this choice (Turns 10 and 12), which leads to Maggie's further statement of 'I like *Beurla* I don't like *Gàidhlig*', which in turn prompts Seumas to weigh in on the conversation (Turns 16, 24, and 26) and question Maggie's assertion that she does not like Gaelic. Seumas then supports Nana in her endeavor to read the story in Gaelic with his encouraging statement of 'a:h *leugh ann a(n) Gàidhlig e Nana*' ('read it in Gaelic'), which orients to the Gaelic-centred FLP in both form and function. As discussed in the 2014a article, this is viewed as a manifestation of Seumas' latent pro-Gaelic ideology; further, this orientation has been brought about by Maggie's overtly negative stance towards Gaelic. Additionally, the Observer's Paradox seems to play a role in bringing this ideological stance to fruition: in realising that he and his family are 'on stage' so to speak, Seumas orients to the view that it is important to maintain Gaelic. Once Nana begins to read 'Little Teddy Left Behind' by Anne Mangan in Gaelic, Maggie does not seem to mind and even uses Gaelic in producing the words *timcheall* ('around'), *fliuch* ('wet'), and *gealach* ('moon') during the storytime interaction. By insisting on reading the story in Gaelic, Nana ensures that an interaction type that is both linguistically and emotionally important to Maggie's development is not ceded to English. After all, reading a story exposes the child to a different register of language; as well, it is an interaction type that can be particularly conducive to caregiver–child bonding, as Maggie sits on Nana's lap, for example, and the interaction moves from a triadic interaction between Nana, Seumas, and Maggie to one centred on the dyadic interaction between Maggie and Nana. By offering to read the story in Gaelic, therefore, Nana ensures that a specific child-centred context remains a Gaelic one despite the circumstance of the book being written in English.

In the December 2014 recordings, Nana explicitly offers Jacob the choice of English or Gaelic in reading stories from the 'Little Alfie Collection' by Shirley Hughes. However, as seen below, unlike the 'Little Teddy Left Behind' interaction in 2009, Nana immediately acquiesces to Jacob's choice to have the story read in *Beurla* ('English', which again, is an ironic code choice for the child given the content of what they are

DOI: 10.1057/9781137521811.0009

saying and which is perhaps even more ironic considering Jacob's overall extremely low use of Gaelic):

EXAMPLE 4.7   *Bonting*

1	Nana	uh *seo* Bunting- Bonting (1.4) 'S *E*:: <u>Bon:ting</u> (2.8)
		here's it is
		'n leugh mi ann an Gàidhlig e no ann am Beurla?
		should I read it in Gaelic or English
2	Jacob	nn - em (.) WH< *Beurla*=
		English
3	Nana	=*Beurla* (.) Bonting (2.6) one fine sunny morning- s::ummer morning

Although Nana's capitulation to English when reading the story is an isolated incident, I argue that it is also indicative of the premise that speakers' orientation to the Gaelic-centred FLP has weakened over time. Here, Nana quickly acquiesces to Jacob's request to have the story read in English and therefore the child does not receive the benefit of being exposed to a different register of Gaelic nor does he take part in an emotionally close activity through the medium of Gaelic. However, it is important to emphasise that the very act of offering to read a story written in English in Gaelic is important in terms of Gaelic's status within the home, as this act presents Gaelic as an equally viable language to use in an important child-centred activity such as storytime. Further, Nana manages to incorporate the use of Gaelic into the interaction by using Gaelic for story-related questions, as seen in the following excerpt:

EXAMPLE 4.8   *Reading the paper*

1	Nana	sitting in the garden having a cup of tea-
		/*dè bha iad a' \dèanamh?* (1.5) *dè bha Grandma a' dèanamh?*
		what were they doing? what was Grandma doing?
2	Jacob	reading the paper
3	Nana	*leughadh a' ^phàipeir*
		reading the paper

In this example, Nana uses Gaelic to ask Jacob a question about the story and then re-casts his English-language response into Gaelic. She thus still orients to the Gaelic-centred FLP despite ceding the actual

DOI: 10.1057/9781137521811.0009

story to English overall. It is postulated that, as discussed in the last chapter, of the three children, Jacob appears to have harboured the most unfavourable attitudes toward Gaelic at a young age. Later on in the interaction, I manipulate the conversation somewhat by asking Nana to read one of the other Little Alfie stories in Gaelic. Nana does so, but within a few turns, Jacob adamantly insists that he wants the story in English, first with 'no I don't want it like this,' then as Nana continues in Gaelic, with an emphatic whining 'no,' followed by 'I don't want it in Gaelic,' which is followed by 'I want it in English.' Jacob then repeats this statement and Nana then switches to English for the remainder of the story. This is paralleled in another interaction in the December 2014 recordings where Isabel is attempting to read Jacob a children's adaptation of the biblical story of Noah's Ark, also written in English, in Gaelic. Jacob, however, objects to reading the story in Gaelic and as in the Little Alfie story interaction with Nana, Jacob repeatedly interrupts Isabel in her Gaelic rendition of the story, declaring that he does not want the story read to him in Gaelic and emphatically commanding Isabel not to continue reading in Gaelic. Isabel finally acquiesces to Jacob's overt request to use English, and like Nana, Isabel tries to incorporate the use of Gaelic in other ways, such as singing a song about Noah's Ark in Gaelic, to which Jacob also objects, and she also uses Gaelic in asking story-related questions, to which Jacob sometimes objects. Although there may be other contextual factors in Jacob's objections to Gaelic being used in storytime, such as the fact that the singing was not actually part of the story, in many ways both the Little Alfie and Noah's Ark interactions from the December 2014 recordings encapsulate the observation drawn from the last chapter that each child is 'less Gaelic' than the previous child. When I first came to the family in 2007, I recall David happily engaging with a story about polar bears written in English while Nana rendered it in Gaelic and do not recall any strife over language choice. He also even engaged at some level with a story with no pictures in it in Gaelic (Nana had translated a story I had written about seals into Gaelic), which shows his willingness to be read to in Gaelic, as there was nothing else to occupy him but the story. In the storytime interaction with Maggie, however, there was clear strife over language choice and she clearly wanted the story read to her in English. However, once the story began in Gaelic, she accepted this language choice and also used Gaelic in engaging with the story. In Jacob's case, not only did he not want the

DOI: 10.1057/9781137521811.0009

stories read to him in Gaelic, but when the caregiver did indeed use Gaelic for storytime, he objected so strongly that the caregiver had to use English or else the storytime interaction would have not taken place. He also sometimes objected to Gaelic being used in *interaction as a whole*, as suggested by his protests against the Gaelic singing and some of the story-related questions.

This last point – that family members are unable to orient to the Gaelic-centred FLP because the child actively precludes them from doing so – plays a central role in the next section, as in conceptualising FLP in terms of *agency*, it is important also to consider the child's agentative role in this process. This section will discuss how in addition to the child's role in this process, certain diachronic and synchronic realities of language shift in the family contribute to the overall unravelling of the Gaelic-centred FLP.

How the FLP is dismantled

Although maintaining the dual-lingual/parallel mode paradigm requires effort on both the part of Peigi and Nana and is also the main way in which they reify the Gaelic-centred FLP, it is important to emphasise that this practice is analogous to Lanza's (1997) 'Move On Strategy', whereby the parent does not directly attend to the child's use of mixing/ non-preferred code choice. This strategy is the penultimate stage on the continuum towards negotiating a bilingual context and as discussed in the introduction, Lanza argues that high use of discourse strategies that negotiate a more *monolingual* context are more likely to result in the child's competence in the minority language, writing that 'strategies for opening negotiations of a monolingual context contribute to *establishing* bilingualism in the early years' (p. 317, emphasis the author's). Thus, while maintaining dual-lingualism means that Peigi and Nana provide an important source of Gaelic input for the children, the reality is that Peigi and Nana do not often negotiate the more monolingual contexts needed for minority language maintenance. This observation is not intended to imply that Nana or Peigi have a *laissez-faire* attitude toward the Gaelic-centred FLP or undermine their commitment to trying to create and maintain a Gaelic-speaking family but rather, a way of understanding how the Gaelic-centred nature of the FLP is dismantled at the

DOI: 10.1057/9781137521811.0009

micro-level. As will be discussed further in this section, the fact the dual-lingual/parallel mode has been established as the modus operandi between Nana, Peigi and the children in the first place signals the beginning of this dismantlement process.

In the December 2014 interview, it is actually Seumas who brings up the concept that more monolingually oriented strategies may be more conducive to raising his nephews and niece as Gaelic speakers. In discussing how his own use of Gaelic with the third generation has changed over the seven years, he highlights the agency the children have in terms of language choice and how this agency in turn reflexively shapes his own language practices with them:

> I speak less Gaelic now than what I did seven years ago (0.4) but the only reason I <u>was</u> speaking it was to encourage David to speak it (1.2) if the <u>children</u> had (1.2) or like Jacob for example was- was speaking Gaelic I would converse to <u>him</u> in Gaelic ... but he just point blank refuses (0.9) maybe it's <u>my</u> fault I should've just maybe spoken to him more in Gaelic and ignored him (.) if he replied back in English but ach that doesn't really work either (.)

The need to discuss the agentative role that *children* play in potentially shaping how a particular FLP is reified (and subsequently dismantled) is highlighted in recent work (see Lanza, 2007; Gafaranga, 2010, 2011) and Seumas' comment clearly illustrates how the children's own language use can in turn influence caregivers' language practices (which is also eluded to in Isabel's comment discussed earlier in which she described dual-lingualism with David as getting her 'hackles up'). Seumas further contemplates the potential impact that invoking a more monolingual strategy when speaking to Jacob – such as not answering when Jacob speaks English – may play in Jacob's acquisition and use of Gaelic. Seumas however concludes that this strategy 'doesn't really work.' As will be further elaborated in this section, Seumas is correct in his hypothesis and one of the reasons for these realities is Seumas' own linguistic practices with adult interlocutors.

In setting up the Gaelic-centred FLP, the adults' goal is for the third generation to become active Gaelic speakers. Gaelic is therefore the preferred language for the children to speak to their caregivers, especially to Peigi and Nana, who are putting a considerable amount of effort in maintaining the Gaelic-centred FLP. However, as gleaned from the previous chapter, all the Campbell children developed a preference for English at an early age: in David's case, this preference was clearly established by age five at the latest and in Maggie's case, by the age of three at the latest. Jacob appeared to exhibit a clear preference for English concurrently with his ability to speak. This early-established preference means that in the case of Jacob (and to some extent, Maggie when she was younger), it may be unrealistic to expect the child to answer in Gaelic because he or she does not have the required linguistic competence. Further, the early establishment of preference would mean that in order to invoke more monolingual strategies, Nana and Peigi would need to constantly either ignore the children's utterances in English or consistently mark them as 'faultable.' Doing so often would not only potentially disrupt communication, but accreted use of these strategies may also possibly impede building close family relationships. In Palviainen and Boyd's (2013) study of Swedish-Finnish families, for example, one mother reports that she ceased using monolingual strategies such as repetition with her second child because she found it 'too exhausting' (p. 235) to maintain. Similarly, Peigi and Nana might also find it 'exhausting' and monotonous to continually correct the third generation's code choice. Therefore, over the years, Peigi and Nana appear to have struck a compromise between the need to maintain a happy family and the need to maintain Gaelic within this family: Nana and Peigi will actively use Gaelic, but they will not insist that the children do so as well. They simply 'move on' from the child's use of the dispreferred language.

Further, in the case of Maggie and Jacob, once dual-lingualism became established with David, the possibility of invoking more monolingual strategies with the younger children greatly diminished. After all, it would be very hard for Nana or Peigi to feign Gaelic monolingualism with Maggie and Jacob when they clearly understand what David says in English. It would also be more difficult for caregivers to remark on the appropriateness of the younger child's language choice, as the younger child can see that the majority language *is* acceptable as evidenced by the fact that the older sibling is not constantly being corrected. These barriers to using more monolingual strategies are not only brought about by Nana and Peigi's interactions with David, but by the interactions in the family as a whole, most notably between Nana and the second generation. As discussed in the previous chapter, dual-lingualism is often the format adopted when Nana speaks to her own children. This is exemplified in the following three short excerpts, which are drawn from a dinner time interaction between Nana, Seumas, Isabel, Maggie, and me in the 2009 corpus:

EXAMPLE 4.9 *Dual-lingualism between Seumas and Nana*

1	Nana	*an d' fhuair thu dhèanamh?*
		did you get it done?
2	Seumas	yeah' I'm going to see about the driver's disk
		I've got that she should have given me that before=
3	Nana	=oh BR<aye>BR
	•	
1	Nana	*cuin a tha thu a' dol sìos?*
		when are you going down?
2	Seumas	she's going to Dingwall tomorrow
		there must be some (?) thing on
3	Nana	oh aye
	•	
1	Seumas	[[you're bringing in any]
2	Nana	[[*shiud thu*]
		there you are
		cuiridh tu thu fhèin a-mach à obair
		you'll put yourself out of work
		ma tha thu ag /innseadh sin do dhuine
		if you tell that to anyone
	(2.0)	
3	Seumas	a:ye
4	Nana	{mmm}
5	Seumas	prob[[ably]
6	Nana	[[mmm]
7	Seumas	well I don't tell it to everybody obvious-
8	Nana	=no I kno:w no

Parallel to the argument that it would be difficult to invoke monolingual strategies with Maggie and Jacob because dual-lingualism has already been established with David, so too would Nana's practices with her own children make monolingual strategies with any of her grandchildren problematic. In looking at these excerpts from the third generation's point of view, it is clear that Nana is not a monolingual Gaelic speaker and that she understands what her son is saying to her. Secondly, Nana does not sanction her son's use of English in response to her Gaelic first-pair part. This therefore suggests to the child that not only is it acceptable to respond in English when addressed in Gaelic, but the fact that the person engaging in this practice is an *adult* may further compound the appropriateness of this practice from the child's point of view. Further, the fact that this interaction

DOI: 10.1057/9781137521811.0009

occurs between a parent and her child may mean that at some level, Nana and Seumas inadvertently model to the third generation that English is the appropriate code for *children* to use *to* their parents/caregivers. After all, the only instance in which the third generation see 'children' use Gaelic to their parents is when they witness their mother Peigi or Peigi's sister speak to Dolina in Gaelic. Further, the final excerpt in this three-part example evidences the observation made earlier that Nana often takes up her interlocutor's code choice of English as a means of orienting to a same-medium preference. Thus, by witnessing Nana's conversations with other adults, the children are observing several interactional norms: first, that a Gaelic first-pair part does not require a Gaelic second-pair part; secondly, that English may be the appropriate code for *children* to use; and thirdly, that persistence in the use of English is likely to result in Nana's eventual switch to English.

'Talking language shift into being' at the micro-level

This last observable norm – switching to the majority language following the interlocutor's use of the majority language – is analogous to the 'Code-Switching' stage in terms of Lanza's (1997) continuum, which Lanza asserts is the strategy that *most strongly* negotiates a bilingual context. Lanza (p. 266–267) demonstrates main two types of code-switching that may occur: lexical insertions into the preferred language (for example, p. 266 where Siri's mother says 'The girl is *borte*, yeah [gone]') or code-switches for the entirety of the following utterance, as seen on p. 267, where Tomas' mother switches to Norwegian following his utterance in Norwegian. Although Nana and Peigi generally tend to uphold the dual-lingual/parallel mode paradigm when speaking to the children, there is evidence that they also employ this most bilingual strategy of 'Code-Switching' when speaking to the children. An example of the first type of code-switching according to Lanza's paradigm can be seen in the following conversation between Nana and Jacob, which is drawn from the interaction shown earlier in the chapter where Nana, Jacob, and I are driving to a restaurant for lunch. Here, Jacob refers to a rocky shoreline in a harbour as a 'beach' and Nana contests this use of the word 'beach,' as seen below:

EXAMPLE 4.10   *Beach*

1	Jacob	can we go to the beach Mommy?=
2	Nana	=*chan eil* beach *a tha seo idir* oh (?)=
		that's not a beach at all
3	Jacob	=yes there is!

DOI: 10.1057/9781137521811.0009

In this example, Nana inserts the English word 'beach' into her Gaelic utterance. In doing so, not only does she orient to the most bilingual context on Lanza's continuum, but it is argued that by taking up Jacob's single lexical item, Nana is conferring a type of legitimacy on his word choice and the language used for this particular lexical item. In isolation, this example may seem relatively trivial; however, over time, this repeated practice, coupled with prevalent mainstream discourses about Gaelic's lexical 'deficiencies' due to it being a 'old-fashioned' language,¹ that Jacob will encounter as he grows older and therefore more metalinguistically aware, compounds its significance. Further, in arguing that the dual-lingual/parallel mode requires Nana to take a 'stand your ground' approach in terms of language choice, it is possible that Jacob may interpret Nana's use of a single lexical item in English as a chink in her linguistic armour so to speak and perceives that persistence in using English may be more likely to result in Nana's eventual capitulation to English in extended turn sequences. This practice of switching to English for extended turn sequences has previously been referred to as Nana's use of 'code-drifting' and this is similar both to the second type of code-switching discussed in Lanza (1997) and also to Gafaranga's (2010, 2011) concept of 'talking language shift into being.' Despite Nana's adherence to the dual-lingual/parallel mode paradigm with her grandchildren, code-drifting to English does occur in conversations between Nana and her grandchildren, not just with Nana's English-dominant adult interlocutors. This is illustrated in the following example, which is again drawn from the interaction in the car where Nana, Jacob and I ('R' in the transcript) are driving to the restaurant:

EXAMPLE 4.11   *Did you see me?*

---

1   Nana   *..a chaidh air a' bhus (.) fac' thu Liz-*
              who went on the bus (.) did you see Liz-
              am fac' thu mise is Liz an-dè ann a shiud? (.)
              did you see me and Liz yesterday over there?
              am fac' thu sinn a' coiseachd nuair a bha thu a' dol a shnàmh? >no cà robh
              did you see us walking when you were going to swimming? or where were
              chan eil fhios a'm an robh thu a' dol ann an a shnàmh
              I don't know if it was to swimming
              a bha thu a' dol shuas an seo idir< =
              you were going at all up here
2   Jacob   =you there?=
3   Nana   =did you see me?

4	Jacob	[[no]
5	R?	([[*chan fhaca ach*]?)
		didn't see but
6	Nana	*am faca Mamaidh mi?*
		did Mommy see me?
7	Jacob	no
8	Nana	no
9	Jacob	no one did see you
10	Nana	<u>no one</u> did
11	Jacob	everyone was asleep
12	Nana	everyone was asleep

Nana's use of English here is interpreted to serve as a medium repair. In this particular excerpt, Nana is speaking very fast, especially when she begins on what appears to be a strand of self-talk after the word *snàmh* in the third line of her Turn 1. The utterances following the word *snàmh* are also for the most part said under Nana's breath.[2] Prior to this strand of self-talk, Nana has asked Jacob the same questions three times, each time elaborating further on her question. However, Jacob does not respond to any of these questions and it is only after Nana's strand of self-talk that Jacob appears to finally engage with Nana's question. Nana then enthusiastically cuts in with her question again, this time using English, to which Jacob replies in English. In the prior dual-lingual/parallel mode conversation examples, it was postulated that the children's responses could be interpreted as medium requests, and further, that these requests could be interpreted to mean that the child has not understood what has been said in Gaelic. However, in maintaining the dual-lingual/parallel mode paradigm, Nana ignored these implicit requests. Here, however, Nana appears to have yielded to Jacob's implicit medium request. It is postulated that the reason Nana yields at this particular juncture and not at others is that she realises that her utterance in Turn 1 is 'fault-able.' Nana's switch to English in 'Did you see me' in Turn 3 therefore is analysed as an attempt to make amends for her 'faultable' utterance and to do so, she uses her interlocutor's preferred language. This repair quickly solves the issue of comprehensibility, as Jacob then immediately answers her question. Nana then switches back to Gaelic in asking Jacob another question, to which he also responds in English.

For the remainder of this excerpt (Turns 8–12), Nana uses English exclusively in repeating or nearly repeating everything that Jacob says. It

DOI: 10.1057/9781137521811.0009

is postulated that this too serves a type of repair sequence; Nana's repetitions show that she is paying attention to Jacob and that the conversation is now on his terms, whereas previously Nana had been the one directing the conversation through her use of questions. Ceding the conversation to Jacob's terms is also interpreted as Nana's attempt to make amends for her faultable utterance in Turn 1. In participating in the conversation on Jacob's terms, therefore, Nana adopts his preferred medium of English, thereby inadvertently 'talking language shift into being.'

This 'talking language shift into being' coinciding with repetitions also occurs in conversations with the older children in the family. The is illustrated in the following excerpt from the 2014 corpus, where Nana, Peigi, David, Maggie, Jacob, and I are at Peigi's house and Maggie is telling us about her day at the *Fèis*:

EXAMPLE 4.12   *Over the sea something something*

1	Nana	@@@@
2	R	*chan eil e=* it's not
3	Peigi	*=tha e toirt beagan ùine nach eil?* it takes a bit of time doesn't it?
4	Nana	*tha* it does
5	R	*tha: tha:* it does it does
6	Nana	*bidh sgiamhail gu leòr ann roimhe nach bi?* there's a bit screeching before isn't there?
7	Maggie	((humming Skye boat song))
8	Nana	((joins in humming))
9	R	((joins in))
10	Maggie	I've got that stuck in my head now
11	Nana	it's stuck in your head
12	Maggie	((humming))
13	Nana	((humming Skye boat song))
14	R	((joins in))
15	Peigi	*an e siud a bha sibh a' dèanamh?* is that what you were doing?
16	Nana, R Maggie	((humming))
17	Peigi	*(càite? air a' [[bhocsa?)]* where? on the box [accordion]?

DOI: 10.1057/9781137521811.0009

18	Nana	[[*bocsa*] box
19	Maggie	over the sea something something
20	R	yeah
21	Nana	over the sea something something @@
22	R	@@ over a s- (.) over the sea to (0.3) *càite?* where?

As can be seen from this excerpt, the adults all use Gaelic, but in Turns 11 and 21, Nana takes up Maggie's code choice of English in a near-repetition and then repetition of Maggie's utterances. I also take up Maggie's code choice in the initial part of my Turn 22, then switch back to Gaelic for the coda of my turn. In this particular excerpt Peigi maintains monolingual use of Gaelic; however, like Nana, in other instances Peigi also lets the dual-lingual/parallel mode paradigm break down and participates in the process of 'talking language shift into being.' Although in isolation this example may appear relatively trivial in terms of overall language shift, as was previously discussed in the 'Beach' example, by switching from Gaelic to English even at the lexical level, Nana confers a sense of legitimacy on the child's code choice. This accumulated legitimacy over various interactions then makes it nearly impossible for Nana to ever invoke more monolingual strategies and either overtly or implicitly critique the child's use of English. Further, like the previous example, Nana's repetition of the child's utterances shows interest in the child's utterances on the child's terms. As so many of the children's utterances are oriented toward gaining the caregiver's attention and approval, as well as autonomy within the conversation, an unintended consequence of these repetitions is that the child is subliminally rewarded for use of English. Further, Nana often repeats the child's utterance when she is particularly amused by it, as exemplified in this excerpt with the repetition of 'over the sea something something' followed by laughter, and it is argued that this indexing of amusement further subliminally rewards the child for use of English.

Unlike the other examples, this example contains no 'trouble spots' that could be interpreted as medium requests due to proficiency/comprehensibility issues. In postulating why Nana is repeating the child's utterances (and on the child's terms by using English), it is necessary to look at Nana's motivations in terms of the children's life trajectories as they have grown older. Before Maggie and David entered school, they

DOI: 10.1057/9781137521811.0009

spent the majority of their time either at home or with their grandmothers; in many ways, the children's primary caregivers (Peigi, Nana, and Dolina) were the centres of their respective universes. Both children were extremely close to Nana and even though they are still close to her now, their worlds have greatly expanded from their interactions within the home environment. To maintain a close relationship with her grandchildren, Nana draws on a range of strategies. Some of the strategies in this repertoire include giving the children attention and autonomy in the conversation through her repetitions, as well as indexing her amusement at what they are saying. As the children are English-dominant, these strategies take place through the medium of English. Further, as will be discussed in greater detail in the next chapter, as English is clearly their preferred language, as well as the one that for them functions as the language of solidarity, other instances of Nana 'talking language shift into being' can be analysed as a way of building solidarity with them as a means of maintaining close relationships with them. Further, as the children progress to adulthood, it may seem increasingly more natural for Nana to use more adult language practices, such as code-drifting, with them.

Attempting to reverse language shift

The previous section discussed how the second generation Campbell siblings' use of English plays an important role in dismantling the Gaelic-centred FLP as set up by Nana and Peigi. However, it has been clear at points in the corpus, as well as in various comments made to me over the years, that the second generation Campbells do in fact wish to arrest the ongoing language shift within their family. For example, as mentioned earlier in the chapter, during David's early years, Seumas stated that the sole reason he used any Gaelic was to assist in David's acquisition of the language. However, this chapter has shown that Seumas' own language practices, such as answering his mother in English when she addresses him in Gaelic, play an important role in how language shift is modelled to the third generation and how this reflexively perpetuates the ongoing language shift. To abstain from these shift-modelling practices would require a significant transformation of linguistic norms on the parts of all speakers within the family. First, the English-dominant members

DOI: 10.1057/9781137521811.0009

would have to make the effort to speak Gaelic in the first place and then the Gaelic-dominant members, such as Nana, would have to treat this use of Gaelic as a normative linguistic practice. Although it may seem strange that given her devotion to the Gaelic-centred FLP, Nana would not treat her own children's use of Gaelic as normal, I draw an example from the pilot recordings in April 2009 to illustrate my point. This was the first recording that involved Seumas and Seumas had mistakenly thought that when the recorder was on, he was only meant to speak in Gaelic. We were sitting down to a meal prepared by Isabel and Seumas asked, *An do rinn thusa seo?* ('Did YOU make this?'). The unnaturalness of Seumas using Gaelic with his aunt elicited so much laughter from everyone in the interaction (Seumas, Isabel, Nana, and I) that I had to turn the recorder off because all it would have captured was hysterical noise. Six years later, it is still a joke among the four of us to say *An do rinn thusa seo* and then start laughing. Over time, with increased persistence, Seumas' use of Gaelic with his adult relatives would become more natural, as after all, Peigi managed to negotiate a complete norm-reversal in her interactions with her sister and mother. The point to be made here in discussing this example, however, is that the act of speaking Gaelic in order to reverse language shift would require a significant amount of effort on the part of *all* Campbell family members and a significant change of well-established norms within the family.

The children's perceptions of RLS attempts in the family

Further, as the point of the FLP is for the third generation members to acquire Gaelic, they too would have to accept the second generation members' use of the language as a normative practice. One potential difficulty with that is that throughout the children's lives, the second generation have always been known as English speakers. For example, as previously discussed, in the 2014 corpus, Màiri tried to use more Gaelic both when speaking directly to the children and also to Nana in the presence of the children. However, Maggie clearly does not view Màiri's use of Gaelic as normative, as at one point on the last night of recording, when Màiri claims *bidh mi a' bruidhinn Gàidhlig* (I [habitually] speak Gaelic) and emphasises this with *an-còmhnaidh* ('often'), Maggie laughs and insists that Màiri normally speaks English. Maggie then re-iterates this point by saying to me, 'she normally talks English.'

DOI: 10.1057/9781137521811.0009

Maggie's understanding of English as Màiri's habitual language is further demonstrated in the following excerpt:

EXAMPLE 4.13 *Why are you talking Gaelic*

1	Maggie	CR< why are you all talking Gaelic?
2	Nana	*a bheil rùm gu leòr agad a ghabhail gin dhiubh*
		is there enough room for you to take one of them
3	Maggie	WH< why
4	Nana	WH< (?)
5	Màiri	yeah
6	Maggie	CR< are you talking Gae:lic
7	Màiri	*uill [[chan eil Beurla againn*
		well we don't speak English
8	Nana	*[[((sings)) tha mi sgìth- chan [[eil Beurla againn]*
		I am tired I don't speak English
9	R	*[['s mi leam fhìn]*
		I'm alone (song lyrics)
10	Maggie	*tha*: Nana you- you <u>always</u> *bruidhinn Beurla*
		yes speak English

In addition to her use of Gaelic in Turn 7, Màiri has been using Gaelic both to Maggie and to Nana throughout most of the interaction. Nana in turn has been using Gaelic with Màiri. Maggie however clearly finds this use of Gaelic unnatural and comments on it, asking why the two interlocutors are speaking Gaelic. Maggie uses Gaelic in first arguing that her interlocutors do indeed speak English (*tha* in Turn 10) and then in a very amusing code-mix in which she insists that Nana always speaks English (also Turn 10). (It is interesting, given the observation made in Chapter 3, that Maggie is still inserting Gaelic lexical items into her English while arguing with her caregivers). This is the only instance in which I've ever heard Maggie question Nana's use of Gaelic and it is clear to see from the other excerpts in this book that, contrary to what Maggie says, Nana does not 'always *bruidhinn Beurla*' ('speak English'). What seems to be different here is Nana's use of Gaelic with *Màiri*, supporting the claim that although Nana may start off in Gaelic with Màiri, she usually 'drifts' into Màiri's preferred code choice of English and further, that Gaelic use between Nana and Màiri is not normative. This illustrates the multiplex challenge that Màiri or Seumas would face in attempting to change their language practices to make a positive impact on the Gaelic-centred FLP and participate in creating a *Gaelic-speaking family*: first, they would have

DOI: 10.1057/9781137521811.0009

to instigate the change; secondly, the adult interlocutors such as Nana would have to *treat* Màiri or Seumas' use of Gaelic as normative; thirdly, the children would have to *view* Màiri or Seumas' use of Gaelic as a common practice, not one that goes strongly against the vein of Màiri and Seumas' habitual language use; and finally, the children would have to perceive that other adult interlocutors' use of Gaelic *with* Màiri and Seumas is normative practice. Clearly, to effect this change would require multiple actors in cooperation with each other and demonstrates how once certain language shift-perpetuating norms are already established within the family, re-negotiating them in order to positively impact the minority language-centred FLP involves much more than certain individuals increasing their use of the minority language.

Proficiency issues

In Màiri's case, the amount of effort needed to change her linguistic practices is also exacerbated by her perceived Gaelic proficiency issues. This is exemplified in the following excerpt from the 2014 recordings, where Màiri has just relayed to me how she thinks she and her partner 'should' use Gaelic but that she prefers to use English with him because he often corrects her Gaelic. The topic of correction then has turned to Màiri's perception that Nana also corrects Màiri's Gaelic:

EXAMPLE 4.14   *You just correct me*

1	Nana	I only correct you [[that's the way that]
2	Màiri	[[you're the] <u>worst</u>
3	Nana	I just- I just <u>quietly</u> repeat=
4	Màiri	you just correct me so I won't make a fool of myself
5	Nana	I just quietly repeat what you shouldn't=
6	Màiri	quietly?
7	Nana	quietly
8	R	@@@@@
9	Nana	that's what uh=
10	Màiri	<u>see</u> [[Cassie I told you you thought I was joking]
11	Nana	[[that's the teaching method]

Despite the light-hearted tone of this excerpt, it demonstrates the difficulties Màiri would face in trying to use more Gaelic in her daily life. As discussed in depth in Armstrong (2013), this phenomenon is not

DOI: 10.1057/9781137521811.0009

uncommon among lapsed Gaelic speakers such as Màiri and it invokes a vicious circle of low Gaelic use: lapsed speakers' diachronic low use of Gaelic has led to language attrition and so when these speakers *do* attempt to use Gaelic, indicators of this attrition, such as grammatical or phonological deviations from a perceived norm, are treated as 'mistakes' and corrected by more fluent speakers, such as Nana. This in turn leads to a lack of confidence and lack of willingness to use the language, as not only may these speakers feel inadequate in using Gaelic to communicate, but the experience of being criticised by family members may not be conducive to maintaining family harmony and close relationships. Additionally, this particular excerpt demonstrates the didactic stance, for example, 'that's the teaching method' in Turn 11, that Nana often takes vis-à-vis Màiri's Gaelic use, which may be due in part to Nana's professional experience as a GME teacher. Although Nana's motivation presumably stems from a desire to help Màiri regain her fluency, it appears to have the opposite effect, as Màiri consequently does not use the language out of fear of saying something incorrectly and then possibly being corrected.

The challenges of reflexivity and RLS

In terms of talk directed at the children, the children's own agency and their high use of English also are a significant barrier to arresting the process of language shift within the family. As highlighted throughout the chapter, speaking to the children in Gaelic while they answer in English is difficult for a number of reasons and Peigi and Nana are the only speakers who seem to be able to sustain this practice for a significant amount of time. Speaking Gaelic to the children is made even more difficult by what is best described as an interactional irony in terms of attempting RLS in the family: because the third generation generally use English, the adults generally do not expect the third generation's utterances to be in Gaelic and therefore do not respond appropriately using Gaelic. This bears resemblance to Kulick's (1992, p. 215) observation mentioned in the introduction that in Gapun, 'the association between children and Tok Pisin is, in fact, so strong that adults will address children in that language even if a child should actually happen to answer in Taiap.' This similar reality in the Campbell family means that sometimes a child's Gaelic utterance is unintentionally marked as problematic because the adult is not expecting a Gaelic utterance and therefore has

DOI: 10.1057/9781137521811.0009

not linguistically processed it correctly. This observation is illustrated in the following example drawn from the 2009 corpus, where Seumas is fixing a computer and Maggie wants to know if it is Seumas' computer or not:

EXAMPLE 4.15   *New 'puter*

1	Maggie	is that your new 'puter?
2	Seumas	*chan e coimpiutair aig Seumas idir a th' ann*
		it's not Seumas' computer at all
		coimpiutair aig boireannach eile
		[it's] another woman's computer
	(2.1)	
3	Maggie	*dè a tha sin?*
		what's that?
4	Seumas	mmm?
5	Maggie	/dʲi ʃɪn/
		(i.e. *dè sin*, 'what's that?')
6	Seumas	*dè?*
		what?
7	Maggie	*dè a tha siud?*
		what is that?
8	Seumas	*dè a tha siud? coimpiutair briste*
		what is that? a broken computer
9	Maggie	no it's not

It is clear from this example that in conversational terms, Maggie is not rewarded for her use of Gaelic. It appears that Seumas does not understand Maggie's Gaelic question in Turn 3, as he answers it with a request for clarification 'mmm?' in Turn 4. Again using Gaelic, Maggie then subsequently modifies her question in Turn 5, the result of which is a very non-standard pronunciation. This is also met with a request for clarification (Seumas' *dè* ['what'] in Turn 6). Maggie then further modifies her question, this time using the deictic *siud*, which denotes an object further away than the deictic *sin* ('that'). Finally, Seumas appears to understand Maggie's question and supplies her an answer (which she subsequently argues against, a phenomenon which seemed a constant feature of her interactions in the 2009 corpus). It appears therefore that Maggie's use of Gaelic has inadvertently impeded her objective of obtaining a satisfactory answer to her question, as Seumas' two requests for clarification delay him answering Maggie's initial question in Turn 1. Further, by making a request for clarification, Seumas is marking Maggie's utterance as 'faultable' and as the two instances in which he makes these requests for clarification occur after Maggie has used Gaelic, it is argued that these requests for clarification may inadvertently give Maggie the impression that her *language choice* is somehow 'faultable.' It is hypothesised that although Seumas uses Gaelic in his Turn 2 (the content of which is clearly confusing to Maggie, as Seumas refers to himself in the third person and then uses *boireannach eile* 'another woman' instead of the expected *cuideigin eile* 'someone else'), Seumas does not initially process Maggie's utterance as Gaelic because he is not expecting her utterance to occur in Gaelic. Thus, Seumas is unintentionally perpetuating the process of language shift at the micro-level by inadvertently offering Maggie a disincentive to speak Gaelic. Throughout the 2009 Corpus, there are several examples of adults (even Nana) not understanding Maggie's Gaelic presumably because they do not expect her to speak Gaelic and it is argued that the adults' subsequent requests for clarification may be a further perpetuating factor in Maggie's low use of the language.

Summary

This chapter has highlighted the reflexive nature of language shift in the family, showing how the shift-inducing practices already in place, such the second generation members' use of English with Nana, further help induce shift in the third generation, and then how this shift further reflexively strengthens the shift already in place, for example, the adults' reluctance to use Gaelic with the third generation because the children respond in English. It has shown how reversing language shift in the family would require more than simply using a higher amount of Gaelic with the third generation; in essence, it would also require transforming the linguistic practices of the adults when speaking to each other. However, it is unclear that if this change were to take place, whether or not it would be accepted by the children as a normative practice. The chapter has also underscored how even though dual-lingualism takes considerable effort on the part of Nana and Peigi, who appear to be the only family members capable of maintaining Gaelic use with the third generation, this practice is actually the tip of the dismantlement process, as it means that Nana and Peigi are unable to negotiate more monolingual-centred strategies with the third generation. In summary, this chapter has shown how the intricate interworking of family dynamics and the progression of language shift make the task of maintaining a minority language with the youngest generation a very difficult task.

Notes

1   It is a common popular myth that Gaelic lacks lexical items for technology and modern concepts, a belief that relates the historical low prestige of Gaelic and its association with backwardness and a rural lifestyle, as well as until recently, its exclusion from the education system.

2   At the time, I may not have understood Nana's self-talk, as from my response in Turn 5, I seem to think that Nana is asking a question of me, not of Jacob. In listening back to the recording, I think that because the self-talk is said so quickly and under her breath, when Nana suddenly says 'Did you see me?' very loudly, I mistakenly think that she is asking a question of me because I am not entirely sure what she has said for part of Turn 1.

DOI: 10.1057/9781137521811.0009

5
Authority, Solidarity, and Language

Abstract: *This chapter examines the reflexive relationship between the family and the community in formulating the argument that the third generation are socialised into language practices that lead to an association of Gaelic with authority and English with solidarity. In particular, it emphasises the role that the gaps where Gaelic is not spoken further strengthens this dichotomy of languages along the authority versus solidarity axis. The chapter argues that these associations create a negative emotional valence for Gaelic and a positive emotional valence for English, which, in addition to the language shift-inducing realities discussed in the last chapter, is a further contributing factor to the children's early and continuing preference for English.*

Keywords: language and authority; language and emotional valence; language and solidarity

Smith-Christmas, Cassie. *Family Language Policy: Maintaining an Endangered Language in the Home.* Basingstoke: Palgrave Macmillan, 2016. DOI: 10.1057/9781137521811.0010.

Aonghas' authoritative stance

One of the main ways that Gaelic becomes the authoritative code within the Campbell family is through Aonghas' linguistic practices, whereby he limits his use of Gaelic primarily to displays of authority vis-à-vis his children. In the 2009 corpus, 14 out of Aonghas' 20 Gaelic/Mixed turns said directly to either Maggie or David occur in conjunction with taking a stance of authority towards them. This authoritative stance consists either of issuing Maggie or David a direct command, for example *cuir sin dhan a' bhin* ('put that in the bin') or in disciplining them for inappropriate behaviour, for example, *sguir do ghearan no chan fhaigh thu càil* ('quit your whining or you won't get anything'). Closer examination of these authoritative uses of Gaelic reveal that Gaelic is often adopted as a last resort strategy, similar to the way a parent might use the child's full name in indexing 'real trouble,' so to speak. This observation is exemplified in the following two excerpts drawn from the 2009 corpus. In the first excerpt, Aonghas is trying to ascertain whether or not David has pyjamas at his grandmother Dolina's house, as David is spending the night there later. David, however, does not answer his father's initial two questions and Aonghas then switches to Gaelic in asking his question a final time. In the second example, which is discussed in the 2014a article, Maggie is misbehaving by touching the fireplace, annoying David, and commanding Aonghas not to look at her. Aonghas then uses Gaelic in ordering Maggie to behave and Maggie subsequently uses Gaelic in her response to this admonition:

EXAMPLE 5.1   *Jammies*

1	Aonghas	what did you say now Dave? (0.9) Grannie got jammies?
2	Màiri	now the cake's gone
3	Nana	ah the cake's finished that's the birthday over (.) mmm-hmm
	(0.7)	
4	Màiri	that's the birthday over
5	Nana	mmm-hmm
6	David	I don't care where it should
7	Aonghas	have you got jammies Dave?
	(0.9)	
8	Màiri	thanks for the present Cassie
9	R	[[of course]

DOI: 10.1057/9781137521811.0010

10	David	[[oh boy] that was rubbish
11	Aonghas	*A BHEIL AGAMSA RI BHITH FAIGHNEACHD ORT A-RITHIST (.)*
		do I have to ask you again
		a bheil jammies *aig Grannie [dhut?*
		does Grannie have jammies for you?
12	David	[yes

EXAMPLE 5.2   *Keep away (from Smith-Christmas, 2014a)*

1	Aonghas	no you've touched that already and burnt your fingers (.) keep <u>away</u> from it please
2	Maggie	I did yes-
3	Aonghas	=you didn't do that yesterday you were <u>crying</u> (.) keep <u>away</u>
4	Maggie	Dave
	(1.5)	
5	Aonghas	what?
6	Maggie	not what I said (.) <u>Dave</u> ((stomps foot)) Dave ((humming 2.0))
7	Aonghas	don't do <u>that</u>
8	Maggie	@@
9	Aonghas	it's not funny
10	Maggie	yes it is
11	Aonghas	no it's not
12	Maggie	yes it is (0.7) why you looking at me stop looking
13	Aonghas	I'm allowed to look wherever I want
14	Maggie	is that David?
(2.8)		
15	Aonghas	I'm looking at you because I'm speaking to you (.) *bi modhail*
		be polite (i.e. 'behave')
16	Maggie	I am *modhail*
		polite
18	Aonghas	no you're not

In both examples, Aonghas' use of English is not successful in achieving its goal, as the child is either unresponsive, as is David in the first example, or continues to argue with him, as Maggie does in the second example. In both instances, the use of Gaelic follows a sequence of Aonghas asking a question multiple times (Turns 1 and 7 in the first

DOI: 10.1057/9781137521811.0010

example) or making repeated demands and arguing with the child (Turns 1, 3, 7, 9, and 11 in the second example). In the first example, Aonghas' use of Gaelic in Turn 11 is accompanied by a raised voice. This turn is finally successful in eliciting a response from David and David's response is very meek in comparison to his earlier comments about the video game (Turns 6 and 10). Aonghas' use of Gaelic in the second example appears less successful, as he and Maggie continue to argue, but as will be discussed later, using Gaelic in her response (Turn 16) indicates that at some level, she has comprehended that her father is overtly indexing his annoyance. In both examples, it is clear that Aonghas has become frustrated with the children and that he is drawing on Gaelic as an additional tool in communicating to them that they should heed what he is saying. It is also clear from the examples that to some degree, the children interpret Aonghas' use of Gaelic accordingly and understand that he means business, so to speak, when he uses Gaelic.

From these examples, it appears that Aonghas perceives that Gaelic is particularly effective in disciplining his children. The observation that directives and reprimands may carry more weight in the minority language is not unique to the Campbell family. In other studies, caregivers' threats may go unheeded until made in the minority language, such as Kulick's (1992, p. 217) observation of young children in Gapun; similarly, Luykx (2003, p. 29) observes that in her host household, Spanish commands are less effective than Aymara ones and Spanish commands are followed by their Aymara equivalents or the Aymara word for 'quickly.' Studies of immigrant communities also evidence a preference for the minority language in using directives and reprimands (see for example, Heye, 1975; Zentella, 1997). In her work on emotion and multilingualism, Pavlenko (2004, 2006) considers the hypothesis that use of the minority language may be related to speakers' perception that their L1 is the more 'emotional' language and thus they may prefer it for emotional extremes, such as anger or affection. Although Pavlenko's work as a whole shows that there is not necessarily a simple one-to-one correspondence with language and emotion, it does indicate that many bilinguals may tend to favour their L1 in expressing anger (see for example, Pavlenko, 2006, p. 133). Similarly, Dewaele (2004) shows that even speakers who have undergone L1 attrition often perceive taboo and swear words as more forceful in their L1 than their L2 (see also Harris, Ayçiçegi, and Gleason, 2003). It is possible therefore that although Aonghas primarily uses English in most spheres of his life, he still perceives his L1, Gaelic, to have

DOI: 10.1057/9781137521811.0010

more emotional force than English. Further, it is the language in which he was disciplined as a child and thus he may feel a certain emotional resonance in using the language to discipline his own children, especially in terms of common disciplinary expressions such as *bi modhail* ('behave yourself').

In addition to the possible greater emotional impact factor of commands in the minority language, another dimension to consider is the overall tendency towards monolingual habitual English use both within the Campbell family and the wider community. There are two aspects to this; first, as English is Aonghas' dominant language in terms of use, instances of Gaelic are more 'marked' (*cf.* Myers-Scotton, 1988) and therefore have the ability to attract greater attention (*cf.* also Auer's [1999, p. 321] assertion that 'codeswitching is most salient against a ground which is monolectal'). This potential for attracting attention is compounded by the fact that as has been discussed extensively in the code-switching literature, regardless of the direction of the code switch, for example from majority language to minority language and vice versa, simply alternating languages can operate as a powerful force in attracting the listener's attention (see for example, Auer, 1984, 1988; also Gardner-Chloros, Cheshire, and Charles, 2000), which, as we see in the examples with Aonghas, is part of the problem: the children are simply not listening to him. In Moin, Protassova, Lukkari, and Schwartz's (2013) study of FLP in Finnish-Russian families, for example, one parent specifically mentioned using code-switching for this purpose, reporting (p. 73) 'If the child is not listening properly, he "wakes up" when the language changes.' Further, as Skye is becoming a more monolingual English-speaking community, using Gaelic in public places in Skye increasingly operates as a secret language. As disciplining in public usually involves embarrassment on the part of the caregiver or child or both, it may be seen as advantageous to use a language the many people are unlikely to understand in conducting this particular type of interaction.

In the second example, Maggie takes up Aonghas' use of the word *modhail* and inserts it into her utterance, asserting that she is indeed behaving herself ('I am *modhail'*). As discussed in Chapter 3, Maggie's use of Gaelic often coincides with taking an argumentative stance vis-à-vis her caregivers' displays of authority. It is postulated that Aonghas' use of Gaelic primarily in disciplinary contexts can account in part for Maggie's own use of Gaelic in this manner. As Aonghas does not evidence a high use of Gaelic overall, especially when conversing with his own siblings,

DOI: 10.1057/9781137521811.0010

with whom he primarily uses English, the relatively high use of Gaelic in disciplinary contexts compounds the language's authoritative association. It is not just that Aonghas *uses* Gaelic in disciplinary contexts, but that he *does not use* the language frequently in most other spheres of his life that forges such a strong link between the language and authority. This link in turn is postulated to account in part for Maggie's occasional use of Gaelic in making bids for authority in the 2009 corpus.

It is also argued that this link with Gaelic and authority, especially in the case of being disciplined in the language, results in a *negative emotional valence* towards the language; in other words, the use of the language does not conjure positive or warm feelings in the child. This negative valence then is argued to act as a powerful force in establishing the children's initial and continuing preference for English throughout their lives.

Authority structures and linguistic practices within the family

In addition to Aonghas' use of Gaelic primarily in disciplinary contexts, the children's association of Gaelic with authority also appears to lie in the broader authority structures and their relationship to linguistic practices within the family. In her study of children's language socialisation in the Liard River First Nation community, Meek (2007, p. 34) observes how children's use of the minority language Kaska often coincides with their displays of authority towards one another, such as commanding each other to be quiet. Meek postulates that this linguistic practice is a consequence of the community-wide language shift and the reality that people who speak Kaska tend to be people in authority – for example, elders – and thus Kaska is reflexively created as the language of authority in the Liard River First Nation community. Similarly, it is argued that the Campbell children's association of Gaelic with authoritative contexts stems not only from Aonghas' use of Gaelic in disciplining them, but also from the reality that, like the children in the Liard River First Nation community, the most frequent users of the minority language are also the family members in the highest positions of authority vis-à-vis the children (their mother, both grandmothers, and to some extent their great-aunt Isabel). This authority is endowed both by hierarchical authority within the family in terms of age as well as the relationship to the child in terms of the amount of time each family member spends as the child's primary caregiver, which in turn equates to how strictly the caregivers feel they may discipline the child, as well as the amount of time they spend engaging in these disciplinary acts.

The 'landline users' and authority

This association between Gaelic and family members in authority is most clearly illustrated in the 2009 corpus through a phone conversation between Maggie and Isabel. This was the only recording in the 2009 corpus that was in any way staged; Peigi had told me that Maggie tended to use a high amount of Gaelic when speaking on the phone compared to other contexts. I was intrigued by this observation, so I asked Isabel to call and speak to Maggie. The observation that Maggie uses a higher amount of Gaelic was born out at the linguistic level within the phone conversation; this particular recording contains the only instances of Maggie's complete Gaelic syntactic structures – in other words, full sentences – that are not questions and do not occur in a context in which Maggie wants something of her caregivers or is being disciplined. During the phone conversation, Maggie produces '*bha Sean* okay' (Grandfather was okay); '*tha Sean* okay' (Grandfather is okay.); '*tha sin* easy peasy lemon squeezy' ('that is easy peasy lemon squeezy'). What was most striking about the phone conversation, however, is not the overall amount of Gaelic, but *how* Maggie uses the language: her use of Gaelic sounds remarkably first generation-like in this particular conversation. It is clear that these syntactically complete Gaelic units include English borrowings, but it is argued here that these borrowings make Maggie's use of Gaelic even *more* first generation-like, as it has been previously established that Nana's use of Gaelic when speaking to other adult interlocutors involves a high degree of English borrowings and code-switching. Maggie also backchannels in a way that is remarkably first generation-like by repeating the word *bha* ('it was') with a rise-fall intonation in each use of the word. She also appears to create a first generation identity in other ways besides her use of Gaelic, as at one point she asserts that she needs to 'get B and Bs.' 'Getting B and Bs' – in other words, hosting Bed and Breakfast guests, which the family refer to as 'B and Bs' – is the realm of Nana, Isabel, and Dolina, all of whom run their homes as Bed and Breakfast establishments during the summer. During this particular summer, Peigi also ran a Bed and Breakfast. Thus,

DOI: 10.1057/9781137521811.0010

in using the phone, Maggie appears to be taking on an adult female role and in particular, a first generation role.

Although Peigi is a second generation member, her use of Gaelic often coincides with first generation speaker norms, and thus it is argued that Maggie appears to associate the use of Gaelic with using a landline telephone and more specifically, with a specific group of speakers, referred to as the 'landline users.'[1] In Maggie's family, the 'landline users' are primarily the four female speakers mentioned in the previous paragraph: Nana, Dolina, Isabel, and Peigi, who are also argued to be the speakers in the highest positions of authority vis-à-vis the children. Therefore, it appears that in using a landline telephone, Maggie tries to invoke a landline user identity and that part of this landline identity is the use of Gaelic. In returning to Meek's (2007) observation about the reflexive relationship between minority language use and authority, like the Liard River First Nation children, Maggie's linguistic practices in this excerpt evidence her association of the minority language with a particular set of speakers; as these speakers also occupy the highest places of familial authority, by extension, the link between the minority language and authority is further forged. Although this particular phone episode appears very positive in terms of language maintenance, it is argued that ultimately the association of Gaelic and authority, which generally does not have positive connotations for the child, creates a negative emotional valence between the child and the language, which then may be a further contributing factor to the child's continued low use of the language.

The 'cool' second generation and solidarity

In arguing that Maggie appears to most associate Gaelic with 'landline users,' and in particular first generation landline users, and by extension, with authority, it is possible to see the positive construction of a solidarity code in contrast to the authoritative code within the Campbell family. Although Maggie is very close to her grandmothers and great-aunt, the generational gap as well as their authoritative role in the family means that Maggie is unlikely to see these speakers and by extension, their language, in solidarity terms, which in this context means a sense of similarity; in other words, similarity to Maggie's peer group, and 'coolness' from Maggie's perspective. Further, as discussed in Chapter 3, Nana and Isabel tend to orient to a traditional perspective, which further reduces

DOI: 10.1057/9781137521811.0010

the likelihood that Maggie would see them in solidarity terms. Similarly, the parent-child dynamic means that Maggie is unlikely to see her mother Peigi in solidarity terms. In contrast, Maggie and her third generation siblings are more likely to view the second generation siblings (Seumas and Màiri) in terms of solidarity. Both Seumas and Màiri are 'cool' in the relatively general sense of the word: they are successful in their careers; they use the latest technology; they drive trendy cars; Seumas especially likes sports; they keep up with popular culture and so forth. Further, at the microinteractional level, they tend to engage in more child-centred activities with the children and tend not to be the disciplinarians, as this task is usually left to the parents and/or grandmothers and great-aunt. Thus, both in a broader sense and as constructed within family interactions, Seumas and Màiri are seen as 'cool' and the language that these 'cool' people speak is English, whereas the language that family members associated with authority speak is often Gaelic. Further, the third generation understand that not only do the 'cool' people speak English, but also that these 'cool' people *prefer* to speak English over Gaelic. This is demonstrated in the following example, which includes utterances discussed in the section 'Attempting to reverse language shift' shown in the last chapter, where Maggie rejected Màiri's claim that Màiri 'often' spoke Gaelic. Here, Maggie evidences that she understands the relationship between habitually *speaking* a language and *preferring* it as seen below:

EXAMPLE 5.3   *You normally speak English*

1	Màiri	*uill- uill cha toil /leamsa Beurla idir*
		well well I don't like English at all
2	Maggie	you <u>do</u>
3	R	@
4	Màiri	/no *cha \toil*
		don't like
5	Maggie	yes you do
6	Màiri	/no *cha \toil*
		don't like
7	Maggie	you- you normally speak English
8	Màiri	^no: *tha- bidh mi a' bruidhinn Gàidhlig*
		[I do] I speak Gaelic
9	Maggie	((laughing)) /no=
10	Màiri	=*an-còmhnaidh*
		always
11	Maggie	Eng/lish

DOI: 10.1057/9781137521811.0010

In this example, it is clear that Maggie equates speaking a language (Turn 6 with 'you- you normally speak English') to 'liking' a language (Turns 1–4). As was discussed in the section 'The children's perceptions of RLS attempts in the family,' it is clear that Maggie knows that her aunt Màiri does not often use Gaelic – therefore, in line with Maggie's reasoning that people use languages they 'like,' it would be logical for her to conclude that Màiri does not 'like' Gaelic very much. Thus, by using English, Màiri and Seumas not only model to the children that 'cool' people use English, but also that 'cool' people *like* English. There may also be a reflexive element to the relationship between preference and solidarity; from early ages, the third generation members showed a preference for English. English is also Seumas and Màiri's preferred language; therefore, not only are Seumas and Màiri 'cool' in their own right, but they are 'cool' because they interact with the third generation in a 'cooler' way: by using the third generation's preferred code of English. As well, it is clear from years of observations that although Maggie and David spend a good deal of time bickering with each other, Maggie does look up to David and that Jacob looks up to both his older siblings. Just like the second generation members, the language that these 'cool' older siblings speak is also English, which therefore further strengthens the association between English and solidarity for the younger siblings. Finally, the fact that all these 'cool' people (second generation members and older siblings) *can speak Gaelic*, but actively *choose not to*, may make Gaelic appear even less attractive and may also prompt the children to see Gaelic in a negative light.

The reflexive relationship between preference and solidarity bears similarity to the argument made in the last chapter that dual-lingualism is apt to break down more often as the children grow older because Nana and Peigi are drawing on the third generation's preferred language as a means to maintaining solidarity with them. As well, Nana appears to let dual-lingualism break down as a means of maintaining solidarity with her own children, meaning that inadvertently, Nana and Peigi also play a role in modelling and constructing English as the solidarity code within the home environment. On a similar line of argument, Seumas and Màiri also inadvertently strengthen Gaelic's position as the authoritative code by their occasional orientations to the Gaelic-centred FLP. Although Màiri and Seumas are not authority figures in the same way that other speakers are in terms of family hierarchy or as previously

DOI: 10.1057/9781137521811.0010

mentioned, in terms of their interactions with the children, Seumas and Màiri are adults and thus occupy a place of higher authority than David, Maggie, and Jacob in the family hierarchy. As previously emphasised, Seumas and Màiri's occasional instances of Gaelic use occur in conjunction with directing talk specifically to the third generation. It is argued that this practice reifies Gaelic's position as an adult-*to*-child language, thus reflexively strengthening its association with authority, as again it is speakers in positions of authority who are using the language not to their peers but to interlocutors (the third generation) who have less authority. This reality is further compounded by the dual-lingual conversations discussed in the last chapter, as second generation members (who have less authority vis-à-vis Nana) use English and Nana uses Gaelic until she capitulates to English. As Isabel is Nana's younger sister, even conversations between Nana and Isabel often illustrate this authoritative dimension, as Isabel often uses English while Nana tries to maintain the use of Gaelic before giving up, as seen in the last chapter. Thus, the third generation see Gaelic's status as the authoritative code constructed in a number of different ways in terms of certain speakers' linguistic practices and their particular relationships towards each other. In contrast to this, they see the 'cool' second generation Campbell siblings use English together and consequently see English as the language of solidarity. This perception is then further unknowingly made into a reality when Peigi and Nana let dual-lingualism break down in order to maintain close relationships with the children.

In arguing that Nana and Peigi let dual-lingualism break down in order to maintain solidarity with the children, it is also possible to hypothesise that in some way, the children may relate Gaelic to authority simply because it is the language that Nana and Peigi *insist* on speaking[2] – after all, I refer to the dual-lingual/parallel mode as a 'stand your ground' approach to language choice. As argued in the last chapter, ultimately, the children wish for Peigi and Nana to switch to the children's preferred code of English. Therefore, the insistence on speaking Gaelic and not ceding to the child's preferred code choice of English subliminally compounds this link between Gaelic and authority. Thus, no matter how child-centred the interaction may be, by virtue of using the child's dispreferred language, or occasionally requesting that the child use the dispreferred language, some level of authority is invoked. This presents rather a conundrum in terms of trying to maintain the minority language

DOI: 10.1057/9781137521811.0010

with the child; naturally caregivers believe the best way to maintain a language with a child is by using the language consistently and providing contexts that encourage the use of the minority language; however, once preference for the majority language has been established, use of the minority language becomes a subtle invocation of authority, which may reflexively catalyse the child's desire to rebel against authority through use of the majority language.

The wider community and the authority/solidarity dichotomy

The association of Gaelic with authority and English with solidarity as played out in the Campbell family resonates with use of the two codes in the wider community. In Skye, as in other communities undergoing shift, it is generally the people with more authority – adults, not children – who speak the minority language; after all, language shift *ipso facto* means that the language is less likely to be spoken by younger speakers and therefore by proxy tends to be associated with older speakers. As also seen in the Campbell family, in Skye the adults tend to be *older* adults, which compounds the 'grannie' image of the language and by contrast, the 'coolness' of English. Meek (2007, p. 36) shows how this 'age-graded positionality' may be a powerful force in further perpetuating the language shift already underway, as children see speaking the minority language as something that their grandparents would do and thus refrain from using it with each other.

The role of the media

Moving beyond the immediate community of Skye, media also plays a large role in how English is presented as 'cool' and therefore the language of solidarity among younger speakers. Chapter 4 discussed how reading a book that was written in English in Gaelic was one way caregivers actively resisted reproducing Gaelic's minority status in the home. However, the children's media has never been limited to books, and as they have grown older, and as technology and its availability have also significantly advanced, it would be nearly impossible for children *not* to notice Gaelic's minority status vis-à-vis English in their media

DOI: 10.1057/9781137521811.0010

consumption. There is a large TV and computer in their living room and between the two of them, Maggie and David have a Kindle, an iPod, an iPad, and a mobile phone. In my experience, I have never seen any of the children actively engage with Gaelic media on any of these devices except when they personally have been featured on the Gaelic TV channel BBC Alba. Maggie, David, and Jacob's media life is dominated by English, which is due primarily to the fact that Gaelic media simply is not very available in comparison to English language media and as evidenced by the 2014 BBC Alba report, also not very compelling in comparison to English language media, especially for children David's age. As mentioned in the first chapter, in general, Gaelic media appears to be aimed either at Nana's age group or Jacob's age group, as a number of programmes are either cartoons in Gaelic or created for an older audience. Thus, there is also little that the children's parents find as compelling as English media, meaning that if the parents are watching TV or the Campbells are watching TV together as a family, such as *Saturday Night Takeaway*, their media consumption is in English. Even when interesting Gaelic media is available, it is not necessarily the case that the child wants to watch it; for example, when Maggie was younger, she loved *Peppa Pig* but declared that she did not like the Gaelic version of *Peppa Pig* because she did not like Peppa's voice.

This asymmetry between the lack of compelling Gaelic and proliferation of English media has several ramifications. First, in thinking about the children's media landscape as a whole (taking into account multiple devices, not just the television), the sheer volume of English media compared to Gaelic reifies Gaelic's minority status. Further, if compelling media is considered 'cool' and English has the media monopoly, English is therefore seen as 'cool'; as well, it is the language of pop culture and of celebrities, which compounds the 'coolness' and therefore the solidarity component of English. Also, the fact that Gaelic TV programming tends to be aimed at either young children or older adults additionally compounds the language's authority status similar to the way this reality plays out in the family: the language is something that either old people speak or is spoken *to* children. This is not to deride the efforts of BBC Alba or the gains it has made in recent years but to highlight the challenges of using minority language media as a revitalisation tool and also how media may contribute to the authority/solidarity dichotomy already present in the Campbell household.

DOI: 10.1057/9781137521811.0010

Authority and solidarity within the school

The dichotomy of Gaelic as the authoritative code and English as the solidarity code is also compounded by the children's other main socialising agent: the school. This is achieved by the linguistic practices within the bounds of the school itself as well as at a conceptual level when contrasting the relatively rigid school domain to the more relaxed home environment. This is illustrated in the following two excerpts (shown in the chronological order in which they occurred in the interaction) where Isabel is querying Maggie about her use of Gaelic at school. This particular interaction occurs on the last night of the recordings and I posit that Isabel's motivation for asking these questions may be because the recording process has brought the third generation's low use of Gaelic to the forefront of family consciousness:

EXAMPLE 5.4　*On the free breaks I don't*

1	Isabel	*agus (.) a bheil thu bruidhinn Gàidhlig a's an sgoil?*
		and　do you speak Gaelic in school?
2	Maggie	uh huh
3	R	*fad an latha?*
		all day?
4	Isabel	(can you?) *(1.5) agus carson ma tha thu dèanamh Gàidhlig ma-tha-*
		and why are you doing Gaelic if
		ma tha thu=
		if you
5	Maggie	=on the (0.7) on the <u>free</u> breaks I don't (.) and then on (1.7) then when we're=

EXAMPLE 5.5　*Cause I'm not a school*

1	Isabel	((clears throat)) when the teacher speaks to you in Gaelic in school do you answer in ^English?
2	Maggie	no
3	Isabel	^okay (2.9) so (0.7)
		nuair a bruidhneas cuideigin riut ann an Gàidhlig ann an sheo
		if someone speaks Gaelic to you here
		(0.9) carson a tha thu freagairt ann am Beurla?
		why are you answering in English?
	(dog growls))	
4	Maggie	((1.1) °cause I'm not in school
5	Isabel	^mm
6	Maggie	a::n:::d (0.5) I don't need to speak Gaelic all the time=
7	Isabel	=but you

DOI: 10.1057/9781137521811.0010

Taken together, these two excerpts illustrate how interactional realities in the school strengthen the authority/solidarity dichotomy already present in the family and community. It is evident from the first excerpt that English is associated with Maggie's peer group and interactions outside the classroom, as English is the language that Maggie uses on her 'free breaks'; in other words, English is the language she and her peers *choose* to use while, as seen from the second example, Gaelic is the language they are *required* to use in answering the teacher. This coincides with the observation mentioned in the introduction that in GME schools and units, there is normally a division of labour in terms of language, with Gaelic relegated to the classroom and English the language that the children use socially (see O' Hanlon, McLeod, and Paterson, 2010; Will, 2012; Nance, 2013; see also Hickey, 2007 for a parallel example in Irish-medium schools). As highlighted in O' Hanlon, McLeod, and Paterson (2010, p. 44), many children in GME come from homes where Gaelic is not spoken at all and as illustrated by Maggie and Jacob's linguistic abilities and preferences in their early years, coming from a home even where Gaelic *is* spoken guarantees neither the child's ability in nor preference for Gaelic. Thus, English is generally the language used among GME pupils and by extension, becomes the language of solidarity.

Although Maggie appears to enjoy school as well as excel in it, compared to her home life, school is a more regimented environment with stricter consequences for failing to comply with adults' requests. The school is therefore a more authoritative domain than the home environment and it is argued that the school actually represents the *most authoritative* domain within Maggie's social landscape. Isabel's question in Turn 1 in the second excerpt frames the use of Gaelic in terms of a highly authoritative interaction type (answering the teacher) within this most authoritative context (the school). Maggie's response in Turn 4 not only suggests that Maggie associates the use of Gaelic specifically with school, and therefore with the most authoritative context in her social landscape, but also implies that Maggie's use of English at home may in part be a reaction to how she experiences and complies with authority in school. In Will's (2012) study of language socialisation in a GME school on the Isle of Lewis, failure to respond in Gaelic often elicited admonishment from GME teachers and the use of Gaelic as mandated in teacher-pupils interactions 'subtly created opportunities for rebellion' (p. 119), meaning that students' use of English therefore functioned as a way of distinguishing their personal identities from their school identities. With

DOI: 10.1057/9781137521811.0010

this in mind, it is postulated therefore that Maggie does not only *not* answer in Gaelic in the home because she associates Gaelic with school in general, but also that she specifically associates the use of the language with complying with authoritative norms. At home Maggie enjoys more freedom and part of enjoying and exercising this freedom may the fact that, as discussed in the last chapter, there are no repercussions for her (or other family members') use of English when addressed in Gaelic.

Discursively strengthening the relationship between Gaelic and school

It is also worth noting that Isabel's initial question in the second excerpt, 'Cause I'm not at school,' appears to be motivated by the fact that I have been using Gaelic in asking Maggie questions about her recent trip to Glasgow and she has answered my questions in English. In witnessing this dual-lingualism/parallel mode dynamic, Isabel asks Maggie about her use of Gaelic in school, therefore discursively strengthening the relationship between the use of Gaelic and school. Isabel also draws a similar parallel in the December 2014 recordings in the interaction discussed in the previous chapter, where Jacob refused to have the Noah's Ark story read to him in Gaelic. After asking about why he does not like Gaelic, Isabel asks about his use of Gaelic in school, as seen below:

EXAMPLE 5.6   *I don't want you to read it in Gaelic*

1	Jacob	[[I don't want you to read it] in Gaelic
2	Nana	*dè an t-ainm [[a bh' air a' bhodach?]* what's the name of the old man?
3	R	*[[carson?]* why?
4	Isabel	*carson a (ghaoil?)* why love?
5	Jacob	cos I don't wan:t you to=
6	Isabel	=*eil thu dèanamh Gàidhlig a's an sgoil?* are you doing Gaelic in school?
7	Jacob	no=
8	Isabel	=/no?
9	Nana	*a bheil thu bruidhinn Gàidhlig a's an sgoil àraich?* do you speak Gaelic in nursery school?
10	Isabel	HI< *seo* Chrissie- come on (0.6) *bruidhinn Gàidhlig* Jacob speak Gaelic
11	Jacob	Chrissie's not <u>my</u> teacher

DOI: 10.1057/9781137521811.0010

Similar to the previous example with Maggie, in this excerpt Isabel also discursively forges the link between Gaelic and school, thereby further tying Gaelic to authority. Also like the example with Maggie, in Turn 10, Isabel frames use of Gaelic specifically in terms of the teacher's use, as she names another teacher who works in the school (who though, as evidenced by Jacob's Turn 11, is not Jacob's own teacher), the underlying implication of which is that the teacher, not the children, is the main source of Gaelic use in the school. She also metalinguistically strengthens the bond between Gaelic and authority by commanding Jacob to speak Gaelic, saying *bruidhinn Gàidhlig* ('speak Gaelic') in Turn 10. Also as in the example with Maggie, here Jacob's lack of Gaelic use (in this case, his overt refusal to have Gaelic used *with* him) is met with asking him about his Gaelic use in school (and then, in Turn 10, commanding him to use Gaelic, which also discursively compounds the link between Gaelic and authority). It has been argued throughout this chapter that Gaelic's connection to school and by extension, its connection to authority results in a negative emotional valence. It is seemingly odd therefore that in questioning Jacob's apparent dislike for Gaelic, Isabel brings up an aspect of Gaelic that is one of the main impetuses for this negative emotional valence – the school. However, throughout the years, I have witnessed several echoes of Isabel's implied maxim to the children: 'if you go to a Gaelic school, then you should speak and like Gaelic.' One of these examples is captured in the 2009 corpus, in which David and Maggie have been arguing over who likes Gaelic and who does not (mentioned in Maggie's section in Chapter 3). David has just announced that he does not like Gaelic and Nana responds accordingly:

EXAMPLE 5.7   *Mum doesn't let me*

1	Nana	*ma-tha faodaidh sibh a dhol dhan sgoil Bheurla*
		If so you (pl.) can go to the English [medium] school
		carson tha sibh ag iarraidh sgoil Ghàidhlig a dhol gu sgoil Ghàidhlig
		why do you (pl.) want a Gaelic school- to go to a Gaelic school
2	Maggie	yes I did
3	Nana	mmm? *feumaidh tu dhol gu sgoil Bheurla*
		you must go to an English [medium] school
4	Dave	Mum doesn't let me
5	R	*dè?*
		what?
6	Dave	*chan eil* Mamaidh letting me whatever it's called
		[Mum's] not

DOI: 10.1057/9781137521811.0010

In this excerpt, Nana frames David's announcement that he does not like Gaelic similar to the way that a caregiver might treat a child's announcement that he or she does not like the supper being served: if you do not like it, do not eat it (and therefore go to bed with no supper). Like Isabel in the last example, Nana discursively draws the link between Gaelic and school, and therefore, between Gaelic and authority, not only by the overt indexing of the relationship, but by the framing of it as an implicit threat that if David does not like Gaelic, then he should attend the English-medium school. This threat is hollow, though, as can be seen from David's utterances in Turns 4 and 6, David perceives that his mother would not allow him to go to English-medium school, even if he wished to do so. Therefore, not only is Gaelic associated with school, but the Gaelic-medium school is the school that David *has to* attend despite other options, which adds yet another layer to the tripartite relationship between Gaelic, school, and authority.

David's attempt to use Gaelic in response to my question in Turn 5 is also argued to index his understanding of Gaelic and authority. As discussed in Chapter 3, the few instances of David's use of Gaelic in both corpora coincide with the concept that on some level, David views Gaelic as 'the polite code,' and it is argued that David uses Gaelic in Turn 6 because he wishes to use his 'polite' code with me As also discussed in Chapter 3, one dimension of David's use of Gaelic to coincide with politeness is that Gaelic clearly is the language that Nana and Peigi to want him to speak, and thus in being polite, he uses the code he perceives will most please his caregivers (as well as the researcher, as David is very aware that I am interested in Gaelic and in particular, *his* use of Gaelic). A further dimension of this view of Gaelic as the polite code is related to the association of Gaelic with authority, and in particular, in using Gaelic to index compliance with authority, such as the use of Gaelic in a school context. In the 2014 corpus, David's two instances of Gaelic were said in answer to direct questions I posed to him. Although the conversation is an informal one about his day at the *Fèis*, the fact that I am a non-family member and one whom David sometimes seems to view in a more 'teacher-like' light may mean that in using Gaelic, he is attempting to invoke the polite code with me because of this interactional dynamic. At face value, David's use of Gaelic as the polite code in the 2009 corpus especially may appear at odds with Maggie's use of Gaelic in arguing with her caregivers in the same corpus. However, they are viewed as two sides of the same coin, as in disciplinary contexts, the child has two options: either to argue back or comply with the caregiver's request. At the age of 3;4 Maggie's first recourse is often to outright argue with her caregivers and to use the authoritative code in doing so. At 7;11 David's understanding of how to deal with arguments has matured somewhat. When a disciplinary context arises, he also sometimes invokes the code he associates with authority, but he does this in a way that is intended to mitigate, not exacerbate, the argument.

Unlike his older siblings, Jacob's few instances of Gaelic use do not overtly evidence an association of Gaelic with authority. However, his strong negative attitudes towards the language may be an indication of his association of Gaelic with authority and the negative emotional valence inherent in this association. As discussed in Chapter 3, however, he does appear to be happy to count in Gaelic occasionally, which highlights the paradox of the relationship between the children's association of Gaelic with school, and therefore authority, and the school as a mechanism for language acquisition and therefore by extension, language revitalisation. In many ways, as also discussed in Chapter 3, school appears to have been a very positive force in Maggie's Gaelic development, not only in terms of her linguistic development, but also in terms of fostering positive attitudes toward her minority language, especially since Gaelic is the main way which Maggie engages with literacy. However, this section has highlighted how it is not necessarily that certain people speak the language or that it is used in certain domains which results in this association with authority, but rather, because Gaelic is *not* spoken by a number of people in different domains, the areas where it *is* spoken become more strongly associated with the language. If, for example Gaelic was used in school in peer-to-peer social interactions, or more frequently in the community in general, it is unlikely that Gaelic would have such a strong association with authority and therefore the negative emotional valence that this association entails.

Summary

This chapter discussed how the third generation see the dichotomy of authority versus solidarity constructed not only within their own family, but at the community and wider sociocultural level as well. It is clear that this dichotomy stems not only from the contexts in which the language is spoken, for example, disciplinary contexts and school, but the people

DOI: 10.1057/9781137521811.0010

who speak it, for example, authority figures in the family, adults in the community, and teachers, as well as the way the language is used with and by these people in the contexts in which it is spoken, for example, Gaelic as the compliance code in GME. These realities are the consequences of language shift and unintended ramifications of language maintenance, as it is argued that it is not only that Gaelic *is* spoken in certain contexts that ties it to authority, but the clear gaps where the language is *not spoken* that lay bare this particular connection. These associations in turn result in a valence dichotomy, where Gaelic is negatively emotionally valenced and English in turn is positively valenced due to their respective associations. It is argued that this dichotomy accounts in part both for the third generation's early and continuing preference for English as they grow older.

Notes

1   Nana (and also Isabel if she is there), for example, usually spends about one to two hours on her landline a day speaking to her siblings and/or cousins on Harris, with all of whom she predominantly uses Gaelic and code-switching. No one else, such as Nana's children, will usually use Nana's landline, as they prefer to use their mobiles. In Maggie's own house, Peigi appears to be the primary landline user.
2   Thank you to the participants of the First Celtic Sociolinguistics Symposium at University College Dublin for helping bring this point to fruition.

DOI: 10.1057/9781137521811.0010

6
Conclusion

Abstract: *This chapter draws together the core arguments of this book in order to examine the language policy and planning implications that emerge from the Campbell family's story. It discusses how the dichotomy between the domains in which the minority language is and is not spoken becomes key to understanding why, despite the Campbell children's seeming advantage over OPOL and immigrant community children, the Campbell children still evidence low use of the language. It also highlights how caregivers' use of the minority language is only half the battle, so to speak, in attaining what Fishman (2001, p. 467) refers to as the 'fulcrum' stage of Reversing Language Shift (RLS).*

Keywords: domains; intergenerational language transmission; language policy and planning; reversing language shift

Smith-Christmas, Cassie. *Family Language Policy: Maintaining an Endangered Language in the Home.* Basingstoke: Palgrave Macmillan, 2016. DOI: 10.1057/9781137521811.0011.

The penultimate sentence in my July 2014 recording observation notes reads 'Too many speakers spoil the FLP,' which is clearly intended to invoke the expression 'Too many cooks spoil the broth.' In writing this sentence, I was comparing the Campbell family to OPOL families and postulating that David, Maggie, and Jacob might use more Gaelic if their interactions were limited to conversations with their mother and grandmothers. After all, the other family members not only use more English with the third generation, but their preference for English also means that speakers such as Nana and Peigi often turn towards English, and that additionally, the third generation are socialised into norms and associations that overall are not conducive to minority language maintenance. This hypothetical limitation of the third generation's interactions to Nana, Peigi, and Dolina, however, is not a reality in the Campbell family nor should it be. It is clear from my years of observations that the children have close relationships with multiple family members and that all family members' lives are the richer for these close relationships. The adults in the family are also close to each other and the children witness and take part in the interactions that build closeness (and sometimes distance – they are a family after all!) between the Campbell family adults. Importantly, the children see the role that language – and specifically, *which* language is used – plays in these interactions.

As discussed in the introductory chapter, the main motivation for this particular FLP study has been to uncover the underlying reasons why, despite the apparent advantages over most OPOL and immigrant community children in terms of interlocutors who speak the minority language *and* education in the minority language, the Campbell children use very little Gaelic. Each child after all has evidenced less Gaelic at an early age than the previous child and none of the children currently use much Gaelic at home except for the specific contexts discussed in Chapters 3 and 5. Thus, in this book, I have sought to explore the reasons for these realities, taking the diachronic and synchronic realities in the family as my starting point and then examining how these realities relate to the language shift in the community as a whole.

The diachronic view of FLP in Chapter 3 revealed that the impetus for the Gaelic-centred FLP in terms of David, Maggie, and Jacob was in many ways borne out of the monolingual English FLP in Peigi's own family when she was growing up. Being raised in English by Gaelic speakers served as a major impetus not only for Peigi to learn Gaelic to fluency as an adult, but also to take a very pro-Gaelic stance in multiple facets

DOI: 10.1057/9781137521811.0011

of her life and especially with her own children. The other main force in the current Gaelic-centred FLP is Nana, who also takes a very pro-Gaelic stance in multiple areas of her life and especially with her grandchildren. Nana also tried to maintain a Gaelic-centred FLP with her own children when they were growing up, but the effect of language shift in the community, combined with the effect of the two eldest children moving to the mainland for an extended period of time, meant that English became and stayed their dominant language. Chapter 4 then examined the role that this language shift in the second generation plays in how the Gaelic-centred FLP breaks down at the synchronic level. The chapter discussed that, in addition to explicitly encouraging the use of Gaelic in child-centred contexts, the main way in which Peigi and Nana enact the FLP is by maintaining the dual-lingual/parallel mode with the children; however, this method is also the tip of the FLP dismantlement process, as the establishment of dual-lingualism means that Peigi and Nana are unable to invoke more monolingual strategies when interacting with the children. Further, Nana's dual-lingual paradigm with her own children, as well as her propensity to allow this paradigm to break down, models to the third generation not only that being addressed in Gaelic does not necessarily require a Gaelic reply, but also that persistent use of English eventually will lead to their interlocutor's switch to English. The chapter discussed the reflexive relationship between the third generation's high use of English and other family members' difficulties in using Gaelic with the third generation and further discussed how this element, coupled with issues of Gaelic proficiency and normative English use within the second generation, make it very hard for second generation members to reverse the integral role they play in perpetuating language shift. It was also emphasised that achieving language maintenance would require not only more consistency in talking Gaelic *to* the third generation, but also the transformation of linguistic practices in the family as a whole.

Chapter 5 examined the concept that Gaelic operates as the authority code and English as the solidarity code both within the Campbell family and a wider sociocultural context and how these associations are integral in understanding the third generation's establishment and continuing preference for English. This dichotomy appeared to be borne out of an understanding of who speaks what language, the contexts in which each language is used, and how the language is used in these specific contexts. The chapter argued that Gaelic is established as the authority code by the fact that the other family members in the higher ranks of authority,

DOI: 10.1057/9781137521811.0011

such as the 'landline users,' are the ones most likely to speak Gaelic; by Aonghas' use of the language in disciplining the children; and the fact that Gaelic is associated with school and specifically interactions with the teacher. In contrast, English is set up as the solidarity code by the fact that the younger, 'cool' speakers in the family use English, both within the family and wider community, as well as the reality that English is the third generation's peer group language, as well as the language of mainstream media. It is argued that in addition to the synchronic processes of language shift in the family (which are often the result of diachronic processes of shift, through speakers' lifetimes and in terms of the family as a whole over time), the negative valence as constructed by Gaelic's association with authority and in contrast, the positive valence in terms of English's association with solidarity, is a further contributing factor to the third generation's continuing preference for English.

Overall, the Campbell family's story illustrates the difficulties inherent in attaining Fishman's GIDS Stage 6 – the intergenerational transmission of the minority language in the home – and how these difficulties may take on different dimensions when examined in a particular context. For example, in Fishman's view, some of the major hurdles to Stage 6 lie in what he terms (p. 409) the 'universalizing macro-forces' that erode 'traditional' families and also the 'urban reality' which he juxtaposes with 'simple village life' (p. 408). However, as we have seen with the Campbells, they for the most part are not battling with urbanisation – most of them live in the same rural village after all (although life there is far from simple it should be said) and they also in many ways are a 'traditional' family as well as an extremely close and loving family, the type of family Fishman implies will be particularly suited to maintaining a minority language in the home. In the conclusion (1991, p. 406–410) to *Reversing Language Shift*, Fishman examines Stage 6 primarily from the caregivers' point of view and his recommendations centre on first mobilising caregivers to implement intergenerational transmission and then providing them the means to sustain this implementation (see especially p. 407, 409). What is striking about the Campbell family experience is that (some) caregivers are *already* mobilised for intergenerational transmission in the home and actively trying to sustain it; however, their success with this venture has decreased with each subsequent child. The Campbell's story thus has shown how having caregivers who actively and willingly use the minority language with the children is only half the battle, so to speak, in terms of intergenerational transmission in the home. The children too have

DOI: 10.1057/9781137521811.0011

agency and their agency, such as for example, their continued preference for and use of the majority language, may be pivotal in the caregivers' ability to transmit the language. Further, as Edwards (2010, p. 31) puts it, the domain of the family 'cannot stand in isolation' from other domains (*cf.* also Canagarajah's [2008, p. 173] quote in the introductory chapter). As has been emphasised throughout this book, there is a reflexive relationship between the family and community, which further underscores that while the caregivers' use of the minority language in the home is extremely important to achieving intergenerational transmission, it is only part of the process, so to speak, in ultimately achieving this important stage.

The elucidation of the sociolinguistic realities of the Campbell family and also Skye as a whole gives a very dismal view of language maintenance efforts. However, this rather dim view is not intended to be a critique of the Campbell family's own efforts at the Gaelic-centred FLP or language revitalisation efforts at a wider level. Rather, what the Campbell's story has illustrated is Fishman's (1991) simple yet profound observation that once language shift starts, it is hard to arrest. Any weak point in language maintenance, such as the second generation's establishment of English as their preferred language, subsequently results in more weak points, such as Nana's frequent uptake of English when conversing with her children. Both of these weak points then further contribute to the shift involving the third generation. As well, the book has shown that in the context of language shift, what may be objectively encouraging realities in terms of overall language maintenance, such as the fact that certain speakers such as Nana use the language frequently, or that Gaelic is the medium of instruction in school, may take on discouraging roles in terms of language maintenance, such as the 'grannie' image of the language or its association with authority. The discouraging aspects emanate from the juxtaposition of the contexts in which the majority language *is* spoken and the minority language *is not* spoken; in other words, it is not just that Gaelic is spoken by the Nana that makes it a 'grannie' language, or the fact that Gaelic is spoken in school that compounds its association with authority, but these realities *in conjunction* with other realities, such as the fact that younger speakers do not generally speak Gaelic and the fact that it is rarely used in the wider community. It is like having a particularly large and blank wall; it is not until a small picture is placed on the wall that its size and vastness are truly evident. However, the very nature of language shift and maintenance means that the only

DOI: 10.1057/9781137521811.0011

recourse maintenance efforts have is to keep placing these pictures on the metaphorical blank wall of language shift. Language shift after all is a process by which the minority language recedes from certain domains and in this recession process, the domains in which the language *remains* become even more strongly associated with the language; conversely, language maintenance hinges on the introduction or re-introduction to domains from which it was previously excluded or from which it receded. Like language shift, this dichotomy between the *presence* and *absence* of the language means that the domains in which the language is introduced/re-introduced become more strongly associated with the language. This in theory may not necessarily hinder language mainte-nance, but in practice, this dichotic reality appears to perpetuate shift and hinder maintenance. For example, the fact that Gaelic was excluded from education in Skye during the first generation's childhood meant that Gaelic was more strongly associated with the home and community, which further amplified the already-present low prestige of the language. When GME became available, however, the presence of the language in school did not erase the association with low prestige, but rather, due to the absence of the language in the home/community, the use in this new domain then took on a new meaning: authority. This perhaps lies at the heart of being a minority language in contact with a majority language: by virtue of *being* a minority language, the minority language is always cast in a negative light vis-à-vis the majority language, no matter what new domains the language now encompasses (*cf.* Romaine's [2006] critique of domain regain/introduction in RLS efforts). This particular example of GME in this context also adds another layer to questioning the efficacy of the school as a vehicle for language transmission, which is another (often debated) issue in language maintenance efforts (see for example Fishman, 1991; Baker, 2007; Edwards and Newcombe, 2005; Sallabank, 2013).

Throughout this book, I have focused on the children's experiences as observable realities and I have only touched on the wider realities about the nature of Gaelic and English contact at a national British and Scottish level. To any child growing up in Skye, however, in engaging in public space within Skye as well as anywhere in Scotland and Britain as a whole, Gaelic's minority status is clearly evident. In the context of the Campbell children, the fact that in some ways the homes in which they spend the most time (their own home, Nana's and Dolina's) are semi-public spaces due to the nature of also being Bed and Breakfast

DOI: 10.1057/9781137521811.0011

establishments, English is clearly the majority language, as that is the language of interaction that proprietors will use in speaking with the B and B guests. In terms of wider discourses about the language, not only is Gaelic reified as a minority language in the public sphere, but some wider discourses about the language border on vitriolic, as shown for example in the title of MacKinnon's (2011) report on Gaelic in the mainstream news outlets: ' "Never spoken here", "Rammed down our throats" – the rhetoric of detractors and denigrators of Gaelic in the press.' As they grow older, awareness of these various discourses and how they tie into ideologies held in wider society may play a formative role in how the Campbell third generation view the language. It is also possible that they are already encountering some of these negative discourses and feelings of being minoritised in school, as Nana relayed to me in 2007 that GME children in Skye were often branded as 'The Gaulics' (*cf.* Morrison's [2006, p. 145] characterisation of GME children feeling like a 'different tribe').

However, the focus of this particular study of FLP and how it relates to language shift is situated in the family and particularly in the child's perspectives in the years I have known them, not in the wider sociocultural context of language shift in Scotland. In bringing together the discussion of how various associations with languages are formed, however, coupled with the argument that it is the *gaps* that are most formative in forging these associations, it is possible to compare the situation of David, Maggie, and Jacob to children being raised in OPOL and immigrant community environments. It is argued that what sets autochthonous minority community children apart from OPOL and immigrant community children is the potential way that the associations with the minority language may manifest. Although in OPOL families a language may have multiplex associations, one of the primary associations is the parent who speaks that language. Further, in typical OPOL studies, children are not socialised into the norms of language shift within their families and communities to the extent that the Campbell children are; although OPOL children may see language shift evidenced by their siblings' language use as well as in micro-level linguistic struggles, for example whether or not language shift is 'talked into being,' these realities are not as omnipresent as they are in the Campbell family. Many of the Campbell children's experiences do however bear similarity to immigrant community families, particularly those whose culture and language may be stigmatised by the majority culture. In these families, it

DOI: 10.1057/9781137521811.0011

is likely that the children will see the shift within their own families and within the wider community. Further, the associations due to contrasting the contexts of where the language is and is not used may have the same detrimental impact on immigrant community children's view of the language. However, there are two associations with the minority language that the Campbell children will never have: first, the association of the language with a place where it functions as the majority language. Even if the OPOL or immigrant community child never has the opportunity to visit the country, he or she will know that *somewhere in the world* there is a place where their minority language functions as a majority language. This, as described in Caldas and Caron-Caldas (1992) can be an important force in encouraging the child's use of the minority language. Secondly, neither will the Campbell children ever have the experience of Gaelic as the *only* common means of communicating with a particular interlocutor, as there are no Gaelic speakers who do not speak English. Kopeliovich (2013, p. 270) notes for example that her Hebrew-dominant daughter Rachel no longer treated writing in Russian as a chore once it was established that Russian was the only common code she shared with a pen pal in Germany. This is not to say that the child will *necessarily* speak the minority language or speak it because of these two reasons, as most often, other majority language pressures outweigh the minority language maintenance; however, the point is that these potentially very utilitarian and positively valenced associations are not a possibility in the Campbell family compared to OPOL/immigrant community families. As this book has hypothesised how the various associations the child has with the minority language can have a powerful effect on its use, it is argued that not having the ability to associate the language and its normative use with a majority language context may be another compounding factor in explaining why, in addition to being socialised into the norms of language shift within their family and community, the Campbell third generation do not evidence much use of the minority language, despite their apparent advantage over OPOL and immigrant community children in terms of multiple family members who can speak the minority language as well as the availability of minority language immersion education.

This is not to say that the third generation will always maintain a low use of Gaelic. As has been shown in multiple other studies as well as in this book, FLP is a constantly evolving language dynamic among family members. As mentioned in the introduction, Kopeliovich (2013)

DOI: 10.1057/9781137521811.0011

for example shows how the birth of her fourth child was integral in encouraging minority language use among her three other children. In September 2014, David, Maggie, and Jacob welcomed a new sister into their household. As she did after Jacob was born, Peigi has again told Maggie that 'babies only speak Gaelic' and it appears that Maggie uses some Gaelic with the baby. Even Jacob, who has clear negative attitudes towards Gaelic, calls his sister by a Gaelic term of endearment: *a thasgaidh*. How long this will last, I cannot say, but the point to be made here is that the children's low use of the minority language is not static. In a visit in March 2014, for example, Maggie – the same child who at the age of 3;4 declared 'I like *Beurla*, I don't like Gaelic' when Nana offered to read a book to her in Gaelic – happily read *me* a book entirely in Gaelic. During their lifetimes, certain junctures in the children's lifetimes may motivate them to use the language more, as Pujolar and Puigdevall (2015) show in their concept of *mudes*, that is, changes in linguistic behaviour at various points in speakers' life trajectories. Someday, for example, when the Campbell children move to the mainland for university or when they are raising their own children, Gaelic may take on new, different associations and they may actively choose to use the language that now reminds them of the grandmother they so dearly love and their beautiful island. Only time will tell.

DOI: 10.1057/9781137521811.0011

References

Altman, C., Feldman, Z., Yitzhaki, D., Lotem, S., & Walters, J. (2014). Family language policies, reported language use and proficiency in Russian – Hebrew bilingual children in Israel. *Journal of Multilingual and Multicultural Development*, *35*(3), 216–234.

Anastasi, A., & Cordova, F. A. (1953). Some effects of bilingualism upon the intelligence test performance of Puerto Rican children in New York City. *Journal of Educational Psychology*, *44*(1), 1–19.

Armstrong, T. C. (2013). 'Why won't you speak to me in Gaelic?' Authenticity, integration, and the heritage language learning project. *Journal of Language, Identity & Education*, *12*(5), 340–356.

Auer, P. (1984). *Bilingual Conversation*. Amsterdam: Johns Benjamins.

Auer, P. (1988). A conversation analytic approach to code-switching and transfer. In M. Heller (Ed.), *Code-Switching: Anthropological and Sociolinguistic Perspectives* (pp. 187–213). Berlin: Mouton de Gruyter.

Auer, P. (1999). From codeswitching via language mixing to fused lects: Toward a dynamic typology of bilingual speech. *International Journal of Bilingualism*, *3*(4), 309–332.

Baker, C. (2007). Becoming bilingual through bilingual education. In P. Auer & L. Wei (Eds.), *Handbook of Multilingualism and Multilingual Communication* (pp. 131–154). Berlin: Mouton de Gruyter.

Barron-Hauwaert, S. (2004). *Language Strategies for Bilingual Families: The One-Parent One-Language Approach*. Clevedon: Multilingual Matters.

DOI: 10.1057/9781137521811.0012

Bayley, R., Schecter, S., & Torres-Ayala, B. (1996). Strategies for bilingual maintenance: Case studies of Mexican-Origin Families in Texas. *Linguistics and Education, 8,* 389–408.

Bella Caledonia. (2013). Gaelic Scots and Other Languages. Retrieved 3 October 2013, from http://bellacaledonia.org.uk/2013/10/03/gaelic-scots-and-other-languages/.

Caldas, S. J., & Caron-Caldas, S. (1992). Rearing bilingual children in a monolingual culture: A Lousiana experience. *American Speech, 67*(3), 290–296.

Canagarajah, S. (2008). Language shift and the family: Questions from the Sri Lankan Tamil diaspora. *Journal of Sociolinguistics, 12*(2), 143–176.

Chatzidaki, A., & Maligkoudi, C. (2013). Family language policies among Albanian immigrants in Greece. *International Journal of Bilingual Education and Bilingualism, 16*(6), 675–789.

Conteh, J. (2012). Families, pupils and teachers learning together in a multilingual British city. *Journal of Multilingual and Multicultural Development, 33*(1), 101–116.

Conteh, J., Riasat, S., & Begum, S. (2013). *Children Learning Multilingually in Home, Community and School Contexts in Britain.* (M. Schwartz & A. Verschik, Eds.). Dordrecht: Springer.

Cormack, M. (1993). Problems of minority language broadcasting: Gaelic in Scotland. *European Journal of Communication, 8*(1), 101–117.

Cromdal, J. (2001). Overlap in bilingual play: Some implications of code-switching for overlap resolution. *Research on Language & Social Interaction, 34*(4), 421–451.

Cromdal, J. (2004). Building bilingual oppositions: Code-switching in children's disputes. *Language in Society, 33*(1), 33–58.

Cromdal, J. (2005). Bilingual order in collaborative word processing: On creating an English text in Swedish. *Journal of Pragmatics, 37*(3), 329–353.

Curdt-Christiansen, X. L. (2009). Invisible and visible language planning: Ideological factors in the family language policy of Chinese immigrant families in Quebec. *Language Policy, 8*(4), 351–375.

Dauenhauer, N. M., & Dauenhauer, R. (1998). Technical, emotional, and ideological issues in reversing language shift: Examples from southeast Alaska. In L. A. Grenoble & L. J. Whaley (Eds.), *Endangered Languages: Current Issues and Future Prospects.* Cambridge: Cambridge University Press.

DOI: 10.1057/9781137521811.0012

de Houwer, A. (1990). *The Acquisition of Two Languages from Birth: A Case Study.* Cambridge: Cambridge University Press.

de Houwer, A. (1998). Environmental factors in early bilingual development: The role of parental beliefs and attitudes. In G. Extra & L. Verhoeven (Eds.), *Bilingualism and Migration* (pp. 75–96). New York: Mouton de Gruyter.

de Houwer, A. (2007). Parental language input patterns and children's bilingual use. *Applied Psycholinguistics, 28,* 411–424.

Dewaele, J. M. (2004). The emotional force of swearwords and taboo words in the speech of multilinguals. *Journal of Multilingual and Multicultural Development, 25*(2–3), 204–222.

Döpke, S. (1988). The role of parental teaching techniques in bilingual German–English families. *International Journal of the Sociology of Language, 72,* 101–112.

Döpke, S. (1992). *One Parent, One Language: An Interactional Approach.* Amsterdam: John Benjamins.

Döpke, S. (1998). Can the principle of 'One Person-One Language' be disregarded as unrealistically elitist? *Australian Review of Applied Linguistics, 21*(1), 41–56.

Dorian, N. C. (1981). *Language Death: The Life Cycle of a Scottish Gaelic Dialect.* Philadelphia: Pennsylvania University Press.

Dorian, N. C. (2015). Mutational transfer in East Sutherland Gaelic: 'Có chuireas éis arm a nis?' Paper presented at the 15th International Congress of Celtic Studies, University of Glasgow.

Dumanig, F. P., David, M. K., & Shanmuganathan, T. (2013). Language choice and language policies in Filipino-Malaysian families in multilingual Malaysia. *Journal of Multilingual and Multicultural Development, 34*(6), 582–596.

Dunmore, S. (2015). *Bilingual Life after School? Language Use, Ideologies, and Attitudes among Gaelic-Medium Educated Adults.* Unpublished PhD thesis: University of Edinburgh.

Duranti, A., Ochs, E., & Schiefflin, B. (2011). *The Handbook of Language Socialization.* Malden, MA: Wiley-Blackwell.

Duwe, K. C. (2006a). *Vol. 11 An Eilean Sgithaneach: Trodairnis, Diurinis and Minginis.* Available at: http://www.linguae-celticae.org/dateien/Gaidhlig_Local_Studies_Vol_11_Trondairnis_Ed_II.pdf.

Duwe, K. C. (2006b). *Vo. 12: An Eilean Sgitheanach: Port Righ, An Srath and Sleite.* Available at: http://www.linguae-celticae.org/dateien/Gaidhlig_Local_Studies_Vol_12_Port_Righ_Sleite_Ed_II.pdf.

DOI: 10.1057/9781137521811.0012

Eckert, P. (1989). *Jocks and Burnouts: Social Categories and Identity in the High School*. New York: Teachers College Press.

Edwards, J. (2010). *Minority Languages and Group Identity*. Amsterdam: John Benjamins.

Edwards, V., & Newcombe, L. P. (2005). When school is not enough: New initiatives in intergenerational language transmission in Wales. *International Journal of Bilingual Education and Bilingualism, 8*(4), 298–312.

Evans, M. (1987). Linguistic accommodation in a bilingual family: One perspective on the language acquisition of a bilingual child being raised in a monolingual community. *Journal of Multilingual and Multicultural Development, 8*(3), 231–235.

Fantini, A. E. (1985). *Language Acquisition of a Bilingual Child: A Sociolinguistic Perspective*. Clevedon: Multilingual Matters.

Fishman, J. A. (1971). The sociology of language. In A. S. Dil (Ed.), *Languages in Sociocultural Change* (pp. 1–15). Stanford: Stanford University Press.

Fishman, J. A. (1991). *Reversing Language Shift*. Clevedon: Multilingual Matters.

Fishman, J. A. (2001). *Can Threatened Languages Be Saved? Reversing Language Shift, Revisited: A Twenty-First Century Perspective*. Clevedon: Multilingual Matters.

Fogle, L., & King, K. A. (2013). Child Agency and Language Policy in Transnational Families. *Issues in Applied Linguistics, 19*, 1–25.

Gafaranga, J. (2000). Medium repair vs. other-language repair: Telling the medium of a bilingual conversation. *International Journal of Bilingualism, 4*(3), 327–350.

Gafaranga, J. (2010). Medium request: Talking language shift into being. *Language in Society, 39*, 241–270.

Gafaranga, J. (2011). Transition space medium repair: Language shift talked into being. *Journal of Pragmatics, 43*(1), 118–135.

Galloway, J. M. K. (2012). *Gaelic Education Data 2011-12*. Inverness: Bord na Gaidhlig.

Gardner-Chloros, P., Charles, R., & Cheshire, J. (2000). Parallel patterns? A comparison of monolingual speech and bilingual codeswitching discourse. *Journal of Pragmatics, 32*(9), 1305–1341.

General Register Office for Scotland – 2001 Census. (2005). Retrieved from http://www.gro-scotland.gov.uk/census/censushm/index.html.

DOI: 10.1057/9781137521811.0012

Goffman, E. (1981). *Forms of Talk*. Philadelphia: University of Pennsylvania Press.

Graffman, K. (2014). *Media behaviour among young Gaelic speakers – A comparative study in Scotland, Sweden, and Finland*. Report for BBC Alba. Stockholm: Inculture.

Grammont, M. (1902). *Observations sur le langage des enfants [Observations on the Language of Children]*. Paris: Melanges Meillet.

Grosjean, F. (1992). Another view of bilingualism. *Advances in Psychology, 83*, 51–62.

Harris, C., Ayçiçegi, A., & Gleason, J. B. (2003). Language, taboo words and reprimands elicit greater autonomic reactivity in a first language than in a second. *Applied Psycholinguistics, 24*(4), 561–579.

Heye, J. (1975). Bilingualism and language maintenance in two communities in Santa Catarina, Brazil. In W. McCormack & S. Wurm (Eds.), *Language and Society* (pp. 401–422). The Hague: Mouton.

Hickey, T. (2007). Children's language networks and teachers' input in minority language immersion: What goes in may not come out. *Language and Education, 21*(1), 46–65.

Highland Council/Comhairle na Gàidhealtachd Website. 2015. Gaelic in Schools. Available at: http://www.highland.gov.uk/info/878/schools/18/gaelic_medium_education.

Hill, J. H. (1983). Language death in Uto-Aztecan. *International Journal of American Linguistics, 49*(3), 258–276.

Kasuya, H. (1998). Determinants of language choice in bilingual children: The role of input. *International Journal of Bilingualism, 2*(3), 327–346.

Kenner, C., Ruby, M., Jessel, J., Gregory, E., & Arju, T. (2007). Intergenerational learning between children and grandparents in east London. *Journal of Early Childhood Research, 5*(3), 219–243.

King, K. A. (2000). Language ideologies and heritage language education. *International Journal of Bilingual Education and Bilingualism, 3*(3), 167–184.

King, K. A., & Fogle, L. (2006). Bilingual parenting as good parenting: Parents' perspectives on family language policy for additive bilingualism. *International Journal of Bilingual Education and Bilingualism, 9*(6), 695–712.

King, K. A., & Fogle, L. (2013). Family language policy and bilingual parenting. *Language Teaching, 46*(2), 172–194.

DOI: 10.1057/9781137521811.0012

King, K. A., Fogle, L., & Logan-Terry, A. (2008). Family language policy. *Language and Linguistics Compass*, 2(5), 907–922.

Kirsch, C. (2012). Ideologies, struggles and contradictions: An account of mothers raising their children bilingually in Luxembourgish and English in Great Britain. *International Journal of Bilingual Education and Bilingualism*, 15(1), 95–112.

Kopeliovich, S. (2010). Family language policy: A case study of a Russian-Hebrew bilingual family: Toward a theoretical framework. *Diaspora, Indigenous, and Minority Education*, 4(3), 162–178.

Kopeliovich, S. (2013). Happylingual: A family project for enhancing and balancing multilingual development. In M. Schwartz & A. Verschik (Eds.), *Successful Family Language Policy* (pp. 249–276). Dordrecht: Springer.

Kulick, D. (1992). *Language Shift and Cultural Reproduction: Socialization, Self, and Syncretism in a Papua New Guinean Village*. Cambridge: Cambridge University Press.

Labov, W. (1970). The study of language in its social context. *Studium Generale*, 23, 30–87.

Lanza, E. (1997). *Language Mixing in Infant Bilingualism: A Sociolinguistic Perspective*. Oxford: Oxford University Press.

Lanza, E. (2007). Multilingualism in the family. In P. Auer & L. Wei (Eds.), *Handbook of Multilingualism and Multilingual Communication* (pp. 45–69). Berlin: Walter de Gruyter.

Leopold, W. (1939–1949). *Speech Development of a Bilingual Child: A Linguist's Record*. Evanston: III.

Li, X. (1999). How can language minority parents help their children become bilingual in familial context? A case study of a language minority mother and her daughter. *Bilingual Research Journal*, 23(2/3), 211–224.

Luykx, A. (2003). Weaving languages together: Family language policy and gender socialization in bilingual Aymara households. In R. Bayley & S. Schecter (Eds.), *Language Socialization in Bilingual and Multilingual Societies* (pp. 10–25). Clevedon: Multilingual Matters.

Lyon, J. (1996). *Becoming Bilingual: Language Acquisition in a Bilingual Community*. Clevedon: Multilingual Matters.

Lytra, V. (2012). Discursive constructions of language and identity: Parents' competing perspectives in London Turkish complementary schools. *Journal of Multilingual and Multicultural Development*, 33(1), 85–100.

DOI: 10.1057/9781137521811.0012

MacKinnon, K. (1974). *The Lion's Tongue: The Original and Continuing Language of the Scottish People*. Inverness: Club Leabhar.

MacKinnon, K. (1991). *Gaelic: A Past and Future Prospect*. Edinburgh: Saltire Society.

MacKinnon, K. (2009). Scottish Gaelic today: Social history and contemporary status. In M. J. Ball & N. Müller (Eds.), *The Celtic Languages* (second edition) (pp. 587–649). London: Routledge.

MacKinnon, K. (2011). 'Never spoken here', 'Rammed down our throats' – *The rhetoric of detractors and denigrators of Gaelic in the press*. Report to Bòrd na Gàidhlig, Inverness, and MG Alba, Stornoway, 7th March 2011. (Evidence to Press Complaints Commission, and Leveson Enquiry).

Makihara, M. (2005). Rapa Nui ways of speaking Spanish: Language shift and socialization on Easter Island. *Language in Society, 34*(05), 727–762.

McCarty, T. L., Romero-Little, M. E., & Zepeda, O. (2008). Indigenous language policies in social practice: The case of Navajo. In *Sustaining Linguistic Diversity: Endangered and Minority Languages and Language Varieties* (pp. 159–172). Washington, DC: Georgetown University Press.

McEwan-Fujita, E. (2010). Ideology, affect, and socialization in language shift and revitalization: The experiences of adults learning Gaelic in the Western Isles of Scotland. *Language in Society, 39*, 27–64.

McLeod, W., O' Rourke, B., & Dunmore, S. (2014). 'New Speakers' of Gaelic in Edinburgh and Glasgow. Report for Soillse. Available at: http://www.soillse.ac.uk/wp-content/uploads/New-Speakers%E2%80%99-of-Gaelic-in-Edinburgh-and-Glasgow.pdf.

Meek, B. A. (2007). Respecting the language of elders: Ideological shift and linguistic discontinuity in a Northern Athapascan Community. *Journal of Linguistic Anthropology, 17*(1), 23–43.

Meeuwis, M., & Blommaert, J. (1998). A monolectal view of codeswitching: Layered codeswitching among Zairians in Belgium. In P. Auer (Ed.), *Code-Switching in Conversation: Language, Interaction and Identity* (pp. 76–100). London: Routledge.

Melo-Pfeifer, S. (2014). The role of the family in heritage language use and learning: Impact on heritage language policies. *International Journal of Bilingual Education and Bilingualism, 8*(1), 26–44.

Milroy, L. (1987). *Observing and Analysing Natural Language*. Oxford: Basil Blackwell.

DOI: 10.1057/9781137521811.0012

Mishina-Mori, S. (2011). A longitudinal analysis of language choice in bilingual children: The role of parental input and interaction. *Journal of Pragmatics, 43,* 3122–3138.

Moin, V., Protassova, E., Lukkari, V., & Schwartz, M. (2013). The role of family background in early bilingual education: The Finnish-Russian experience. In M. Schwartz & A. Verschik (Eds.), *Successful Family Language Policy: Parents, Children and Educators in Interaction* (pp. 53–82). Dordrecht: Springer.

Morrison, M. F. (2006). A' Chiad Ghinealach – The First Generation: A survey of Gaelic-medium education in the Western Isles. In W. McLeod (Ed.), *Revitalising Gaelic in Scotland* (pp. 139–154). Edinburgh: Dunedin Academic Press.

Müller, M. (2006). Language use, language attitudes, and Gaelic writing ability among secondary pupils in the Isle of Skye. In W. McLeod (Ed.), *Revitalising Gaelic in Scotland* (pp. 119–138). Edinburgh: Dunedin Academic Press.

Munro, G., Taylor, I., & Armstrong, T. (2011). *The State of Gaelic in Shawbost.* Teangue, Isle of Skye: Bòrd na Gàidhlig. Retrieved from http://www.gaidhlig.org.uk/The state of Gaelic in Shawbost.pdf.

Myers-Scotton, C. (1988). Code-switching as indexical of social negotiations. In L. Wei (Ed.), *The Bilingualism Reader* (2000th edition) (pp. 151–186). London: Routledge.

Nahirny, V. C., & Fishman, J. A. (1965). American immigrant groups: Ethnic identification and the problem of generations. *The Sociological Review, 13*(3), 311–326.

Nance, C. (2013). *Phonetic Variation, Sound Change, and Identity in Scottish Gaelic.* Unpublished PhD thesis: University of Glasgow.

National Records of Scotland (NROS). (2013). *Statistical Bulletin – Release 2A.* Retrieved from http://www.scotlandscensus.gov.uk/documents/censusresults/release2a/Stats.

Ochs, E. (1993). Constructing social identity: A language socialization perspective. *Research on Language & Social Interaction, 26*(3), 287–306.

Ó hIfearnáin, T. (2007). Raising children to be bilingual in the Gaeltacht: Language preference and practice. *International Journal of Bilingual Education and Bilingualism, 10*(4), 510–528.

Ó hIfearnáin, T. (2013). Family language policy, first language Irish speaker attitudes and community-based response to language shift. *Journal of Multilingual and Multicultural Development, 34*(4), 348–365.

DOI: 10.1057/9781137521811.0012

O'Hanlon, F., McLeod, W., & Paterson, L. (2010). *Gaelic-medium Education in Scotland: choice and attainment at the primary and early secondary school stages.* Inverness: Bòrd na Gàidhlig.

Okita, T. (2002). *Invisible Work: Bilingualism, Language Choice, and Childrearing in Intermarried Families.* Amsterdam: John Benjamins.

O'Rourke, B., Pujolar, J., & Ramallo, F. (2015). New speakers of minority languages: The challenging opportunity – Foreword. *International Journal of the Sociology of Language,* (231), 1–20.

Palviainen, Å., & Boyd, S. (2013). Unity in discourse, diversity in practice: The one person one language policy in bilingual families. In M. Schwartz & A. Verschik (Eds.), *Successful Family Language Policy: Parents, Children and Educators in Interaction* (pp. 223–248). Dordrecht: Springer.

Pan, B. A. (1995). Code negotiation in bilingual families: 'My body starts speaking English.' *Journal of Multilingual and Multicultural Development, 16*(4), 315–327.

Patterson, J. L. (1999). What bilingual toddlers hear and say: Language input and word combinations. *Communication Disorders Quarterly, 21*(1), 32–38.

Pavlenko, A. (2004). 'Stop doing that, Ia Komu Skazala!': Language choice and emotions in parent–child communication. *Journal of Multilingual and Multicultural Development, 25*(2–3), 179–203.

Pavlenko, A. (2006). *Emotions and Multilingualism.* Cambridge: Cambridge University Press.

Pillai, S., Soh, W.-Y., & Kajita, A. S. (2014). Family language policy and heritage language maintenance of Malacca Portuguese Creole. *Language and Communication, 37,* 75–85.

Pujolar, J., & Puigdevall, M. (2015). Linguistic mudes: How to become a new speaker in Catalonia. *International Journal of the Sociology of Language, 2015*(231), 167–187.

Quiroz, B., Snow, C., & Zhao, J. (2010). Vocabulary skills of Spanish–English bilinguals: Impact of mother–child language interactions and home language and literacy support. *International Journal of Bilingualism, 14*(4), 379–399.

Rindstedt, C., & Aronsson, K. (2002). Growing up monolingual in a bilingual community: The Quichua revitalization paradox. *Language in Society, 31,* 721–742.

Robertson, B. (2003). Gaelic education. In T. Bryce, W. Humes, D. Gillies, & A. Kennedy (Eds.), *Scottish Education* (pp. 250–261). Edinburgh: Edinburgh University Press.

DOI: 10.1057/9781137521811.0012

Romaine, S. (2006). Planning for the survival of linguistic diversity. *Language Policy*, 5, 441–473.

Ronjat, J. (1913). *Le développement du langage observé chez un enfant bilingue*. Paris: Champion.

Ruby, M. (2012). The role of a grandmother in maintaining Bangla with her granddaughter in East London. *Journal of Multilingual and Multicultural Development*, 33(1), 67–83.

Sacks, H., Schegloff, E., & Jefferson, G. (1974). A simplest systematics for the organization of turn-taking in conversation. *Language*, 50, 676–735.

Sallabank, J. (2013). *Attitudes to Endangered Languages: Identities and Policies*. Cambridge: Cambridge University Press.

Saville-Troike, M. (1987). Dilingual discourse: The negotiation of meaning without a common code. *Linguistics*, 25(1), 81–106.

Schiefflin, B., & Ochs, E. (1984). Language acquisition and socialization: Three developmental stories and their implications. In A. Duranti (Ed.), *Linguistic Anthropology: A Reader* (pp. 296–328). London: Blackwell.

Schiefflin, B., & Ochs, E. (1986). Language socialization. *Annual Review of Anthropology*, 15, 163–191.

Schmidt, A. (1985). *Young People's Dyirbal: An Example of Language Death from Australia*. Cambridge: Cambridge University Press.

Schwartz, M. (2008). Exploring the relationship between family language policy and heritage language knowledge among second generation Russian–Jewish Immigrants in Israel. *Journal of Multilingual and Multicultural Development*, 29(5), 400–418.

Schwartz, M. (2010). Family language policy: Core issues of an emerging field. *Applied Linguistics Review*, 2, 171–192.

Schwartz, M., & Moin, V. (2012). Parents' assessment of their preschool children's bilingual development in the context of family language policy. *Journal of Multilingual and Multicultural Development*, 33(1), 35–55.

Schwartz, M., Moin, V., & Klayle, M. (2013). Parents' choice of a bilingual Hebrew-Arabic Kindergarten for the children. In M. Schwartz & A. Verschik (Eds.), *Successful Family Language Policy: Parents, Children and Educators in Interaction* (pp. 53–82). Dordrecht: Springer.

Silverstein, M. (1979). Language structure and linguistic ideology. In R. Clyne, W. Hanks, & C. Hofbauer (Eds.), *The Elements: A Parasession*

DOI: 10.1057/9781137521811.0012

on *Linguistic Units and Levels* (pp. 193–247). Chicago: Chicago Linguistics Society.

Smakman, D., & Smith-Christmas, C. (2008). Gaelic language erosion and revitalisation on the Isle of Skye, Scotland. In T. de Graaf, N. Ostler, & S. Reinier (Eds.), *Endangered Languages and Language Learning: Proceedings of FEL XII* (pp. 115–122). Leeuwarden: Fryske Akademy.

Smith-Christmas, C. (2012). *I've lost it here dè a bh' agam: Language Shift, Maintenance, and Code-Switching within a Bilingual Family.* Unpublished PhD thesis: University of Glasgow.

Smith-Christmas, C. (2014a). Being socialised into language shift: The impact of extended family members on family language policy. *Journal of Multilingual and Multicultural Development, 5*(35), 511–526.

Smith-Christmas, C. (2014b). Code-Switching in 'Flannan Isles': A microinteractional approach to a bilingual narrative. In R. Lawson (Ed.), *Sociolinguistics in Scotland* (pp. 277–295). Basingstoke: Palgrave Macmillan.

Smith-Christmas, C., & Armstrong, T. C. (2014). Complementary reversing language shift strategies in education: The importance of adult heritage learners of threatened minority languages. *Current Issues in Language Planning, 15*(3), 312–326.

Smith-Christmas, C. & Smakman, D. (2009). Gaelic on the Isle of Skye: Older speakers' identity in a language shift situation. *International Journal of the Sociology of Language, 200,* 27–48.

Spolsky, B. (1991). Hebrew language revitalization within a general theory of second language learning. In R. L. Cooper & B. Spolsky (Eds.), *Influence of Language on Culture and Thought: Essays in Honour of Joshua A. Fishman's 65th Birthday* (pp. 137–156). Walter de Gruyter.

Spolsky, B. (2004). *Language Policy.* Cambridge: Cambridge University Press.

Spolsky, B. (2012). Family language policy – The critical domain. *Journal of Multilingual and Multicultural Development, 33*(1), 3–11.

Spolsky, B., & Shohamy, E. (2000). Language practice, language ideology, and language policy. In R. D. Lambert & E. Shohamy (Eds.), *Language Policy and Pedagogy: Essays in honor of A. Ronald Walton* (pp. 1–42). Amsterdam: Johns Benjamins.

DOI: 10.1057/9781137521811.0012

Stavans, A. (2012). Language policy and literacy practices in the family: The case of Ethiopian parental narrative input. *Journal of Multilingual and Multicultural Development, 33*(1), 13–33.

Taeschner, T. (1983). *The Sun Is Feminine: A Study of Language Acquisition in Bilingual Children.* Berlin: Springer-Verlag.

Takeuchi, M. (2006). The Japanese language development of children through the 'one parent–one language' approach in Melbourne. *Journal of Multilingual and Multicultural Development, 27*(4), 319–331.

The Scottish Council for Research in Education. (1961). *Gaelic-Speaking Children in Highland Schools.* London: University of London Press.

Varro, G. (1998). Does bilingualism survive the second generation? Three generations of French–American families in France. *International Journal of the Sociology of Language, 133*, 105–128.

Walsh, J., & McLeod, W. (2007). An overcoat wrapped around an invisible man? Language legislation and language revitalisation in Ireland and Scotland. *Language Policy, 7*(1), 21–46.

Wei, L. (1994). *Three Generations, Two Languages, One Family.* Clevedon: Multilingual Matters.

Wei, L. (1998). The 'why' and 'how' questions in the analysis of conversational code-switching. In P. Auer (Ed.), *Code-Switching in Conversation: Language, Interaction and Identity* (pp. 156–179). London: Routledge.

Wei, L., Milroy, L., & Ching, P. S. (1992). A two-step sociolinguistic analysis of code-switching and language choice: The example of a bilingual Chinese community in Britain. *International Journal of Applied Linguistics, 2*(1), 63–86.

Wells, G. (2011). *Perceptions of Gaelic Learning and Use in a Bilingual Island Community: An Exploratory Study.* Report for Soillse. Available at: http://www.soillse.ac.uk/wp-content/uploads/Perceptions-of-Gaelic-Learning-and-Use-in-a-Bilingual-Island-Community.pdf.

Will, V. K. A. (2012). *Why Kenny Can't Can: The Language Socialization Experiences of Gaelic-Medium Educated Children In Scotland.* Unpublished PhD thesis: University of Michigan.

Withers, C. W. (1984). *Gaelic in Scotland 1698-1981.* Edinburgh: John Donald Publishers.

Withers, C. W. (1988). *Gaelic Scotland: The Transformation of a Culture Region.* London: Routledge.

Yamamoto, M. (1995). Bilingualism in international families. *Journal of Multilingual and Multicultural Development, 16*, 63–85.

DOI: 10.1057/9781137521811.0012

Yates, L., & Terraschke, A. (2013). Love, language and little ones: Successes and stresses for mothers raising bilingual children in exogamous relationships. In M. Schwartz & A. Verschik (Eds.), *Successful Family Language Policy: Parents, Children and Educators in Interaction* (pp. 105–126). Dordrecht: Springer.

Zentella, A. C. (1997). *Growing up Bilingual: Puerto Rican Children in New York*. Malden, MA: Wiley-Blackwell.

DOI: 10.1057/9781137521811.0012

Index

Note: 'n' indicates note, 't' indicates table

DOI: 10.1057/9781137521811.0013

DOI: 10.1057/9781137521811.0013

DOI: 10.1057/9781137521811.0013

DOI: 10.1057/9781137521811.0013

Lightning Source UK Ltd.
Milton Keynes UK
UKOW01n0012050216

267746UK00003B/12/P